The Instant AI Agency

How To Cash 6 & 7 Figure Checks
In The New Digital Gold Rush
Without Being A Tech Nerd

Dan Wardrope

Copyright © 2024 by Dan Wardrope

All rights reserved. No part of this publication may be reproduced, distributed, or transmitted in any form or by any means, including photocopying, recording, or other electronic or mechanical methods, without the prior written permission of the publisher, except in the case of brief quotations embodied in critical reviews and certain other noncommercial uses permitted by copyright law.

Foreword

Every Thursday for the past four years, Dan Wardrope and I get together over Zoom with my Mojo Mastermind.

We always kick off by sharing our breakthroughs of the week.

Dan is one of the rare members who ALWAYS has at least one breakthrough to unpack.

Dan is forging new frontiers in AI where no man has ever gone before.

He's turned AI into a money-saving and income-generating machine for brick-and-mortar, finance, and e-Commerce businesses by removing the "artificial" from artificial intelligence.

Dan's created the most natural "Sales Android" I've ever seen. I've witnessed Dan's Androids do the work of a staff of salespeople for pennies on the dollar and return 6 figures in sales that would've been lost forever.

This is no small feat.

As the saying goes, "Pioneers take the arrows, settlers take the land."

Dan has already taken countless arrows and shed his own "blood" to figure this out so his people won't have to do battle.

Now, if you love a good sharp arrow to the chest?

If you want to roll around in the mud, blood, and tears?

No need to buy Dan's book.

But…

If you plan on using AI as any type of sales machine and want to save the years, mountains of money, and brain herniating strain Dan has gallantly suffered to bring these pages to you—so you can just "take the land" and profit—you'll be forever grateful you made this tiny investment in your future.

Rooting For You,
Travis Sago
Author of *Make 'Em Beg to Buy from You*

Contents

Introduction 1
   Who's This Book For? 5

Part 1: How It All Started 8
   The Deal That Changed Everything 12
   The Birth Of Flexxable Pay Per Lead 15
   COVID: Economic Change And Challenges 16
   The 2023 Pivot: AI Automation Agency 17

Part 2: The AI Gold Rush 22
   The California Gold Rush Of 1848 22
   The Trillion-Dollar Problem 25
   How AI Is Disrupting The World 30

Part 3: The ROYA System 35
   Controlling Assets Vs. Owning Assets 38
   The Old Way Of Lead Generation 40
   The Typical Ad Agency 45
   The NEW Stress-Free Way To Do Lead Generation 48
      Our Secret Weapon for Higher Booked Calls: SMS 49

Why ROYA Is The Strongest Offer In The Market 58

How David Went From A Struggling Lead Gen Agency To Working With The UK's Top Solar Agency 64

Why Everyone Selling AI Is Going To Fail 66

Story Time: How A 9-5er Quit His Job And Is On Track To Do 8-Figures PROFIT In His First Year 67

How A One-Man Agency From Antibes, France, Closes $22 Billion Dollar Companies 77

How The ROYA System Works 80

The Process 81

    Step 1: The Approach 81

    Step 2: The Coffee Date 82

    Step 3: The Close 83

    Step 4: The Sleeping Beauty Android Build 83

    Step 5: The Prince Charming Kiss 84

    Step 6: The Sales Call 84

    Step 7: Profit 84

    Step 8: Repeat 84

Part 4: Getting ~~Clients~~ Partners 85

Who ROYA Works For (And Best Niches) 87

Selling Principles For Maximum Sales 89

    Selling Principle 1: Widen The Yes Hole 90

    Selling Principle 2: Be Ready To Walk Away 92

    Selling Principle 3: We Are The Prize 95

Selling Principle 4: It's A HELL YES Or A HELL NO 96

Selling Principle 5: Show, Don't Tell 96

The 4-Step Partner-Getting Process 98

Step 1: The Pitch 98

Step 2: The Coffee Date 101

Step 3: The Demo 102

Prompt Instructions 103

Step 4: The Agreement 116

Outreach Methods 118

Warm Network/Referrals 118

Facebook Ads 121

Cold Email 122

Facebook Groups 123

Instagram 126

Joint Ventures 127

Closing And A List Of Deal Structures You Can Use 130

Deal Structure 1: Zero Risk Performance Basis 131

Deal Structure 2: "Zero-ish" Risk Performance Basis 132

Deal Structure 3: Frontend AND Backend Deals 132

Deal Structure 4: Straight Up CHUNKY Retainer 134

Deal Structure 5: Deductible Deposit 134

Get Paid FASTER With Anchor Points 137

Part 5: Delivery And Scaling 140

    Tools You'll Need Access To 141

    Prince Charming Challenge 142

        PCC – Day 1 (Setting Up HighLevel) 142

        PCC – Day 2 (Setting Up Sleeping Beauty Sales Android) . 143

        PCC – Day 3 (The Android Build) 144

    Scaling Up And Upselling The Next Package 145

        Fresh Leads 145

        Speed To Lead 146

        Out Of Hours 148

        Document Collection Android 149

Part 6: The Future Of Lead Generation 151

Part 7: What's Next 154

    SELL FIRST, BUILD LATER 154

    Want To Work With Me To Hit Your First $1k/Week And Build A 6-7 Figure AI Automation Agency? 156

Bonus Chapters 158

    List Of Potential Niches 158

    How To Get Coffee Dates The "Old Skool Way" 162

    How To Build An Agency Website In HighLevel 163

    Checklist For Implementing The ROYA System 164

Useful Links To Start Your AI Automation Agency 167

Introduction

10 years. That's how long it's taken for this book to fully "take form." The lead generation industry, and by extension, the online marketing space, has changed so much during this time that I knew I had to write another book.

In fact, my last book, *Take the Lead*, written back in 2021, has become outdated in many ways. At the time, I had pioneered a new lead generation model called Pay Per Lead (PPL).

This allowed me to basically write my own checks, breaking through any income "glass ceilings" imposed by traditional methods like the retainer model. (If that doesn't make much sense yet, don't worry; I'll explain everything in detail in the following chapters.)

Take the Lead introduced the PPL method and taught thousands of "lead genners" how to implement it, and the result was a wave of new agency owners making life-changing income and finally getting paid what they're worth.

The problem is that the industry has changed.

Not in the sense that PPL doesn't work. It does. It still remains one of the strongest lead generation models out there. If you're looking for a lead generation method for acquiring NEW leads, that is still the method I would recommend.

However, as a model for aspiring online entrepreneurs who want to quit their 9-5s, create "FU money," and give their families the kind of life they've always dreamed of?

I no longer believe PPL is viable nor the best route for making maximum money in minimum time.

Instead, this book tries to fix what *Take the Lead* no longer does. It's everything I wish I had access to if I was starting out again.

Now I know how important your time is. I don't take that for granted! You've put your faith in me by getting this book, and I will deliver. My goal is for you to use the information in this book to achieve your dreams faster than you thought possible.

If I am to summarize what I'd like you to know by the time you finish reading, it is these 3 things:

1. Know, without a doubt, that the opportunity in front of you CAN change your life
2. Have the knowledge and tools to achieve it, and
3. Have the confidence to get out there and make it happen!

This is a big claim! I'm only willing to make it because I've seen firsthand, in my own business and for the hundreds of students I have taught this model, that it can change people's lives.

To demonstrate this to you, I'll spend the first part of this book giving you bags of proof, evidence, and case studies to back up this claim.

In short, I'm going to share one of the biggest wealth opportunities in our generation—a way for anyone to tap into the AI Gold Rush and get paid $10,000, $50,000, even $100,000+ in fees per deal without needing a fancy degree or putting in years of hustle that most business opportunities require.

I'll break down a simple system that allows you to find and partner with big businesses, close them into 6-figure (sometimes even 7-figure) contracts even if you've never done this before, and use AI to reactivate their databases and collect up to 50% of the sales you generate for them.

It sounds ridiculous. You may even think this is a "scam," but I'll explain everything and show you how it all works. You'll see this is all based on proven business principles, solving real business problems for real businesses.

Once you discover how this system works and how easy it is to use, you'll go from hustling and grinding for a "just enough" paycheck to having total control over your time, finances, and freedom.

Now I know what you may be thinking, "This all sounds great, but I don't have any technical abilities or experience with AI."

Let me put those doubts to rest right now. You don't need to be a programmer, data scientist, Harvard graduate, or have any special computer skills. The system I'm going to outline requires zero coding abilities.

All you need is the willingness to follow instructions and put in some effort upfront to get things set up properly, which I'll show you step by step how to do.

Who's This Book For?

This book is for anyone who wants to get paid and get paid WELL, without trading time for money or spending years "working your way up."

It's for the 9-5ers who dream of quitting their jobs one day—who want to start a simple online business and replace their income.

But this book is also for existing online service providers—agencies, freelancers, media buyers—looking for a new performance-based revenue stream and an opportunity to get away from demanding and difficult clients or being stuck in fulfillment.

Even if you're already a business owner—maybe you're in real estate, insurance, solar, dog training, beauty salon, dental, or even e-Commerce—so long as you need leads, you can implement this system in-house to activate your own dormant database and increase revenues while cutting costs.

The opportunity is HUGE (in fact, I believe it's a trillion-dollar industry) simply because every business in the entire world has leads, wants more leads, and wants better leads.

In the coming chapters, you're going to learn how I went from traditional "lead generation" to discovering what I believe is the greatest wealth shortcut of our generation.

You'll learn why this AI Gold Rush is a blue ocean right now and turning average folks into millionaires...

You'll discover our ROYA system and how we're using little things called "Sales Androids" to disrupt household brands without having any "tech" experience.

You'll also learn how to land 50% revenue shares through partnership deals with companies desperate for this solution. They're in a hell of a lot of pain right now with profit margins being squeezed, and this is their savior!

By following this process, you'll be able to replace your 9-5 income, stop trading hours for dollars, and live your dream life.

I'll also give you a 4-step process to land your first client and build your very own AI Sales Android.

The entire process is laid out step by step within these pages. I've made it as easy as possible to follow, and I've included videos for you to watch if you're the visual type.

If you're ready to use cutting-edge technology to make money faster than you ever thought possible, this book will be your guide. The AI Gold Rush is just getting started—all you have to do is stake your claim.

Part 1
How It All Started

My name's Dan Wardrope. I'm the owner of FlexxDigital, my lead generation agency, and Flexxable, my online education company. I didn't come from money or have any special advantages growing up. In fact, I grew up in Australia, found my way over to the UK in 2002, and have remained here ever since.

After getting a degree in chemical engineering, I spent a decade working in the field while also playing semi-professional basketball. My "claim to fame" was leading the 2006 Commonwealth Games tournament in scoring and, the following year, dropping 18 points on Ricky Rubio when we played in Barcelona!

Not too long after that, my knees started going and I had to retire early.

I didn't know it then, but basketball was the only thing keeping me sane in my day job designing sewage treatment plants, of all things!

By September 2009, I was desperate for a change. I turned to Google, typing "how to make money online," hoping to find a way to create a life with more freedom and fulfillment.

In those days, there wasn't a ton of info out there like we have available to us today.

However, what I found exposed me to the world of online marketing, and the idea of being my own boss and living a life of luxury excited me.

I became obsessed, devouring any information I could find. During those early years, I tried:

- Wealthy Affiliate University
- Selling ClickBank products with SEO
- Selling iPhone insurance with SEO
- Starting an SEO business
- The Warrior Forum
- Selling locally grown pot plants
- Launching my courses on The Warrior Forum

It took me a long time to get any kind of success. I don't want to say how much money I lost in the early years trying to make my dream a reality.

It took years of hustling, but I finally landed a big lead generation retainer gig with a non-profit where I was managing $40k/month in Google Ad spend. I was getting great results and doubled my fees when I introduced them to Facebook Ads. Finally, I could taste some success.

But as lucrative as that client was, the retainer model started weighing me down.

If you don't know what a retainer gig is, it's basically when a client pays you a set amount each month for delivering a service.

For example, you could be paid $5k/month to run someone's Facebook Ads for their business. It's a solid gig. The consistent income is fantastic.

And to double your income, all you need to do is take on another $5k/month client, and boom! Now you're making $10k/month! As long as you know what you're doing, it's not too difficult to manage this work.

But while the consistent and almost guaranteed income is great, it's not without problems.

Clients continually delayed payments each month, and soon, I was owed a massive amount. I could be dropped at any moment, and I lived in constant fear that if my performance dropped, I'd be cut the next month and have no way to pay my bills. On top of this, I hated answering to needy clients, texting me at 10 p.m. at night and constantly jumping through hoops while being underpaid for the value I provided. I did this online thing to avoid having a boss, but when I had 5 clients, it felt like I had 5 bosses!

I remember working 80-hour weeks, stuck behind my desk, and yet, no matter how hard I worked, I couldn't crack 6 figures a year.

What's worse, whenever I took on new clients, I'd get so busy I couldn't look after my old clients. Of course, that meant I dropped the ball a few times and would lose an old client, putting me back to square one.

I started to wonder… *how I can scale my lead gen agency, manage more clients, and make more money if every time I take on new clients, I end up losing my old ones?* This is the classic "churn and burn" that happens to every agency owner.

Some try to fix this by hiring staff. But if you hire cheap, their poor work will hurt your clients. If you hire good talent, you kill your profit margins to the point where it doesn't make financial sense anymore.

I knew there had to be a better way.

Then, one day in 2016, a client asked if I wanted to sell them leads on a "cost per lead" basis rather than charging them a monthly fee.

I didn't know it then, but this small shift in my business model would change the entire trajectory of my career.

The Deal That Changed Everything

See, this simple shift was going from charging a fixed fee retainer model to an almost 100% performance-based model.

For example, instead of charging a set fee of $5k/month to manage someone's ads, I would charge a fee for every lead they wanted.

I would generate leads for X amount of money, depending on the niche, and then sell these leads to my clients for 2X or more.

If I wanted to make more money, I could mark each lead up more than 2X or work on reducing my lead cost in order to generate each lead for less.

This was the birth of the Pay Per Lead model, and we discovered it almost by accident!

This new deal structure meant we could make more from one client than we could with 10 retainer clients in one month.

In fact, this little switch in strategy led to my first big win—landing a whale client who paid me $15,000 monthly profit to generate leads on a Pay Per Lead basis.

But the best part was the fact that I was no longer seen as an "employee" under someone's payroll. No one could boss me around or chase me for updates. No one expected me to work a set number of hours, either. Instead, each month, I'd ask my client how many leads he wanted, I'd bill him, turn on the ads, and deliver the leads. That's it! It was a true partnership in a sense.

This is when I knew I'd never trade time for money again. I finally experienced the power of performance marketing.

This first deal showed me the incredible potential of lead generation when you move beyond the limiting retainer model. I became obsessed with this new path, studying and tweaking my lead gen process. It gave me a vision for how to build a truly profitable lead generation business.

In the years that followed, I built a team of 13 employees at FlexxDigital.

We had some incredible achievements.

One of my biggest campaigns was for a finance offer. We ran it on Twitter, and it blew up like nothing I'd ever seen before. In just the first 4 hours, we walked away with $2,598.98.

Of course, we milked it, repeating it over and over again, 7 days a week, until the offer expired.

I later discovered that my leads had generated a mind-boggling $171 million USD for the UK economy, and I was on top of the world.

We became a big player in the lead gen industry, and demand for our services became overwhelming.

The Birth Of Flexxable Pay Per Lead

Once we became a leading player, spending millions mastering Facebook, YouTube, and Twitter ads to generate leads for mega clients, I started to wonder if I could teach others what we were doing with our unique Pay Per Lead process.

So in 2018, I hit go on this idea and launched Flexxable. It was built as a digital education hub, created for those who wanted to create an agency similar to FlexxDigital.

Our students were mainly agency owners, SEO specialists, affiliate marketers, even business owners who weren't making as much money as they'd like and wanted a better way to increase their income.

I'm proud to say that many of the top "lead genners" of today came from Flexxable. For many years, the Pay Per Lead model continued to reign, giving clients better service and agency owners a way to finally get paid what they're worth and enjoy the freedom they deserve.

While Flexxable was a success, I eventually ran into the limitations of the traditional Pay Per Lead model. Rising ad costs, competition, compliance, and market saturation made it increasingly harder to generate leads profitably through paid advertising. That's not to say it doesn't work. It does, and there will always be a place for cold traffic lead generation through social media. But if you were trying to enter this industry as a newbie today, it would be much harder than it was 5-7 years ago.

COVID: Economic Change And Challenges

In the years after 2020, COVID-19 decimated the economy and job market. Businesses slashed spending as consumer demand plunged. Many went out of business. Those who didn't go under tightened their belts, which meant getting them to invest in lead generation was harder than ever before.

See, during any economic downturn, one of the first things businesses stop spending on is advertising. Fewer businesses buying advertising meant fewer jobs going around for agency owners.

The lead generation industry was also going through huge changes with the whole "make money online" idea becoming more popular. This drove hundreds, if not thousands of new people into lead generation, creating huge supply at a time when demand for lead generation was dwindling.

In the years following 2020, lead generation became a much harder business to run—our method of performance-based

Pay Per Lead model made it a bit easier, but it wasn't without its problems as well.

The 2023 Pivot: AI Automation Agency

Thankfully, 2023 gave us a new technology that had the potential to change everything: artificial intelligence.

As soon as ChatGPT came out, we started tinkering with it, seeing how it could improve the way we handle lead generation. Initially, we only used it to write ads like everyone else. But as the months went by and the technology started to mature, my team and I started wondering what else it could do.

As luck would have it, an opportunity landed on our doorstep by a gentleman named Jamie Woods. Jamie came to us, excited that he'd discovered a way to use AI throughout the lead gen process to make everything more efficient. We ended up partnering with Jamie and he's still our top AI expert in the business.

Any lead genner will know that one of the biggest problems in our industry is the point at which we hand over the leads to the client. That's because leads are hottest the moment they come in. Say they opted into a landing page from a

Google Ad to get more information about a loan. They will never be more interested in getting more information (and potentially making a purchase) than at that point. We call this a "hot" lead. In an ideal world, our client will see the lead come into their database and immediately call them to push the sale forward.

How often does this actually happen? Well, if you're working with a small company or just a bad sales team, they may not get in touch for a few hours. Maybe even a day. Maybe more! Every hour that goes by, that lead is getting colder and colder. Meaning the lead "quality" goes down.

So here's what happens next: the client tries to call the lead a few days later and they can't get through. Or they do get through, but the lead is no longer interested or has bought somewhere else. The client then comes back to you... and they complain that **your** leads are crap!

This issue is rampant in the lead gen industry. It also means you can get fired even though you did nothing wrong. We've been trying to fix this "Speed To Lead" issue for years, even trying automated follow-ups, but even then, it requires manual sales staff to re-qualify and book them back into the calendar.

In 2022, we faced a similar problem with a client in the legal niche.

For 6 months, we'd been working alongside a solicitor to enter a new industry. This was to help people get refunds on tax and stamp duty.

After putting in a ton of prep work, we were finally ready to begin the paid ads to bring in leads. Two weeks in, and things were working well, but one day, the client suddenly informed us they wanted to pause everything and cancel the work we were doing. We were shocked. So much work had been put into this, and we were about to have everything taken away. When we inquired further, it turned out the solicitors weren't able to determine if a lead was qualified to get a refund on their stamp duty or not because doing so required understanding and having access to hundreds of case laws to compare against. This task would take hours for a human to qualify one lead.

Instead of throwing in the towel, we wondered if ChatGPT could help here. It had just come out a few months ago, but we knew it was possible to "train" it on case law, and perhaps it could help the solicitors qualify the leads better.

So we got to work and pulled together all the required legal documents to train ChatGPT, along with thousands of case law examples so ChatGPT would be able to cross reference what happened with other people and determine if the lead was eligible for a refund or not.

A couple of weeks later, we were ready to restart the ads. This is how we built the funnel:

1. Run ads
2. Lead hits a landing page and inputs their information into a form
3. ChatGPT sits behind it to run the numbers and spits out a yes/no answer
4. It would then SMS them and either ask more questions or book them into a call

We had no idea if this would work. But as we saw AI having conversations with leads in real time, we were amazed it was actually working. Furthermore, AI could ascertain if a lead was qualified or not about 90% of the time. It wasn't perfect, but it was good enough. This saved our campaign and helped our client make a ton of sales.

Having tasted this early success, we pushed forward and started looking at what else we could automate with AI.

That led us to one of our biggest discoveries that has generated millions between us and our students, database reactivation and the start of the new AI revolution: AI Automation Agencies.

But before I get too ahead of myself, I need to "set the scene" a little more so you fully understand the scope of this AI opportunity in front of us.

Part 2
The AI Gold Rush

The California Gold Rush Of 1848

While overseeing the construction of a new sawmill on January 24, 1848, James W. Marshall, a carpenter and sawmill owner from New Jersey who had moved to California in search of new opportunities, discovered gold flakes in the water.

Marshall was working on constructing the sawmill along the South Fork of the American River near Coloma, California, for businessman John Sutter. While inspecting the mill's progress, Marshall noticed something glittering in the mill's tailrace. He retrieved it and discovered it was flakes of pure gold. Excited by the discovery but wanting to keep it secret initially, Marshall showed the gold to Sutter to obtain his permission first before revealing it publicly.

Word spread quickly, however, and soon, people wanting to cash in on the opportunity were arriving in Coloma to try their luck panning for gold in the river. Many more found visible pieces of gold very nearby. Marshall's discovery was soon confirmed and made public, sparking the infamous Gold Rush. News of the discovery spread via ports and, within months, was making headlines around the world.

This small discovery kicked off one of the most famous wealth-building opportunities in America, The California Gold Rush.

In fact James' find transformed California from a little-populated Spanish territory into a boom state. Over the next few years, it drew hundreds of thousands of prospectors and miners to seek their fortune.

This same type of "gold rush" is happening right now with AI.

It's mid-2024 as I write this book, and we've just gone through 4 years of chaos. It started with the pandemic, which led to one of the biggest stock market crashes in recent history. This was followed by widespread, global economic destruction, the Ukraine war, and a whole host of additional problems.

As a result, people lost their jobs. They spent less money because they had less money. Right now, we're experiencing high interest rates, which is making borrowing more expensive. This is having a knock-on effect, making everyone's loans and mortgages astronomically more expensive, leading to even less disposable income.

The result? Reduced productivity, lower GDP, lower growth, more expensive goods and services, and fewer customers. This was a "perfect storm" for anyone running a business, and that's why we've had more bankruptcies and businesses, especially small and medium-sized enterprises (SMEs), shutting down in the last 4 years.

On top of this, to kick-start growth, governments have been printing cash at enormous rates with no signs of slowing down.

As of right now the US national debt is rising about $1 trillion every 100 days, topping out at $34.4 trillion (though likely much more by the time you're reading this). This is a 90% increase from $18 trillion in 2020, just 4 years ago.

In short, this means inflation is out of control, pumping up the cost of living.

Now, these numbers are so big it's kind of hard to understand what it actually means for the average person.

So here's an easier way to understand this: the average person is worse off, they have less disposable money. This means they're tighter with what they do spend, choosing cheaper options or cutting back altogether.

The Trillion-Dollar Problem

Now, let's look at this from a business perspective since this is what we're really interested in.

If people have less money, they spend less. That means there are fewer leads interested in making a purchase and, ultimately, fewer sales being made.

Compound this lack of sales problem with every single business, in every single country, in every single city, and you can start to see how big of a problem this is.

There's not a single company in the world that wouldn't benefit from more leads and better quality leads.

On top of this, the US economy alone is worth $25.3 trillion. Even if we only take the industries we can conduct lead generation services for, this number would STILL be in the trillions of dollars, and that's not counting every other country we can work in.

Now, with such a big problem, you'd think there are a ton of people out there solving this problem and getting paid well, right? Wrong. There are many people *trying* to do it, but not very well. I believe this is because we're in a global recession, and it's very tough to turn around a business in this kind of economy. That's not to say it's impossible, but you need a very high skill level.

Do you remember my story from Part 1?

I got my start in paid advertising lead generation services, offering Google and Facebook ads. However, with the average consumer tightening their wallets and spending less, it makes sense that they're not clicking on ads to buy things.

If they're not clicking on ads, I would need to target more people, hopefully to convert more prospects into leads. This means I need to spend more on advertising to get the same amount of leads I used to get in a good economy. As a result, the cost of ads goes up.

There comes a point when the cost to acquire a lead is so high that running ads is no longer profitable.

This hurts the agency, which gets fired for poor performance. And this hurts the business because they can't acquire new leads and keep the sales engine running.

But businesses DO still need leads or they'll die, which means running ads is a necessary evil for many of them. This mindset leaves us with business owners who can be highly skeptical and risk-averse when looking to hire lead generation services (or, in fact, any service).

This leads us to the next problem online service providers face: getting clients.

Most agency owners will follow the retainer model. It's the same service I used for many years. This service requires the client to pay upfront for the service and be "locked in" for a specific duration.

However, when we're talking about the average person being worse off and cash-poor, it's not just them affected. It's businesses as well. While not every business has cash flow problems, the economy IS causing them to be more wary of spending the money they do have. And that means it's getting harder to pitch them on lead generation services, especially if you're new and don't have a track record to show.

See, the core pain points of business owners are 1) inflating costs and 2) reduced profit margins. These problems are only getting worse each year that goes by.

Right now, almost all they think about is how much money they're losing and how every decision they make will either make this worse or better.

I speak to agency owners all day, every day, and I hear the same problems when they try to get clients. Their "pitch" is almost always some variation of:

"Hey, Mr. Client, I think I can help you get more leads and increase your sales. All you need to do is pay me $5k/month plus $1k/month in ad spend."

When you do this, their guardrails go up immediately. All they see are flashing red lights: **WARNING: MONEY GOING DOWN THE DRAIN!**

The problem with this pitch is that it's asking for money upfront with no guarantee that it'll return.

It's made worse because most businesses have been burned by agencies before, so they know it's a big, fat risk taking on a new agency only to find out 3 months later the agency can't do its job and the business is now out $20k.

This is why I no longer teach newbies how to do Facebook Ads lead generation. It's just too hard. To make a decent living, you need to be very good at what you do and have a track record to show.

That's the bad news if you don't have years of experience and a proven track record.

The good news is that there's another way to cash in on this trillion-dollar problem and help businesses solve their sales problems without having bags of experience or technical knowledge. And, of course, get paid handsomely, which is what we're all interested in.

In the following chapters, I will show you how to position yourself to solve this trillion-dollar problem—and give you the tools to do it.

When you start to see how you can do this yourself and that there is virtually zero competition on what we do (for now), along with being able to target the biggest markets in the world, it will change everything for you.

If you're reading this and somehow we've made it out of a recession and the economy's thriving, what I'm about to share with you is still relevant.

In my years of doing this, I've discovered that there are timeless problems you can solve that will always be in demand. If you can make it rain for companies and help them make more SALES, you will always have food on the table!

How AI Is Disrupting The World

Now that we understand a little more about the market we're in, business owners, and their problems, we can start considering how to come up with a solution.

This is marketing 101. We find a market. We find a pain point. We provide a solution. If that solution solves their problem in a unique, clearly different way using a desirable concept, we have a winner.

Once you understand this, you'll know how to craft powerful pitches that open doors and close all the clients you want.

When you think about what business owners are really buying from a lead gen service (or any service), it's not more leads, it's not the person doing the service, it's not even results. It's certainty.

When they part with their hard-earned cash, they want to know there's a good level of certainty it will come back to them (and hopefully more).

The problem with a new agency is that there's nothing to give businesses the certainty they're looking for. In fact, their pitch is often a generic offer they've heard a million times, is full of holes, and leaves them feeling MORE uncertain.

The thing is, all of these feelings of uncertainty come down to one thing and one thing only:

Humans.

Humans are prone to making mistakes, they let things slip, they get hungry, tired, stressed, anxious, fearful... the list is endless.

The problems are compounded when you have an inexperienced person running the show.

But what about AI?

While it's not perfect either, it has many plus points.

AI doesn't get hungry, it doesn't take days off, it doesn't get tired, it doesn't get stressed, and as long as you give it the right direction and guidance, it will stay on track and get the job done.

That's why when you rely on a consistent, reliable, efficient robot to do a job, and demonstrate that it works, certainty of results goes up.

But that's not all.

Because AI is much cheaper and can do a better job than most humans in specific jobs, it not only helps reduce costs by freeing up staff to work on higher-level tasks or replacing them entirely but also increases profit margins.

That means AI robots fulfill the 2 "bleeding neck" pain points that business owners have.

And this is the biggest difference between AI-driven agencies and human-driven agencies.

By selling this (and demonstrating AI can do the job), we can give clients certainty, land huge household names, and get paid $100k+ per contract, all during a "recession."

Now, before we wrap up this chapter, I want to finish off the story that started this AI Gold Rush chapter. See, despite

James W. Marshall's discovery of gold, he actually ended up dying penniless.

He didn't own the land and failed to create a mining company to take advantage of the hidden gold.

Only a very small percentage of the hundreds of thousands of people made decent money during the Gold Rush.

In fact, one of the first millionaires was a man named Samuel Brannan. Samuel worked for the local newspaper at the time, and he made the first public announcement.

He then purchased all the mining supplies in San Francisco, walked through the streets, and proclaimed, "Gold! Gold! Gold from the American River!" This alerted everyone to the opportunity, and because he owned all the local mining supplies, he sold them off and made an absolute killing.

I love this lesson. It's not the ones who use AI that will be rich (some will, most won't), but the ones who sell the AI "shovels!"

This is what we're doing with AI Automation Agencies.

We're helping companies who don't have the ability, knowledge, or resources to use AI become AI-powered almost overnight, and that's a huge selling point for folks who want to be seen as innovative without taking on the risk of doing it.

This is your opportunity to "sell the shovel."

Part 3
The ROYA System

Now you have a better understanding of my background and the AI revolution we're staring down the barrel of, I can tell you more about what we're doing to take advantage of this opportunity and dominate the market so we're "set for life."

To do that, we use a system called ROYA.

ROYA stands for **R**ent **O**ut **Y**our Sales **A**ndroid.

We coined the term "Sales Android" because that's exactly what it is: an AI-powered, human-like robot that makes sales! We have many different kinds of Androids that do different things, and I'll introduce you to them later on.

We're not just building an AI chatbot. There are hundreds of them on the market. Ours works better than anything available right now (June 2024), and paired with our unusual way of negotiating DEALS, we can earn 1,000 times more than someone selling an "AI chatbot" for $97 per month.

Now before we get too far ahead of ourselves, I do want to drive home here that technology is moving at lightning speed right now. It's very likely by the time you read this, a few of the "techy" parts of this system may change and we may have better tools that do what we're trying to achieve faster and easier.

For example, voice AI is coming along leaps and bounds right now. We believe it will soon become an incredible tool for us to use.

That said... the overall philosophy behind what we do will NOT change.

If I am to summarize exactly what we do for our partners (not clients—more on this later), it is this:

Every business has dead leads sitting in its database. Leads the businesses spent good money on and will never get back. This is costing the industry BILLIONS in lost sales.

With our AI Sales Android, we turn your dead leads into new SALES automatically—without any upfront costs, even if they've been dialed to death by your sales team already.

Make sense so far? I'll go into this process in more detail coming up. In essence, we achieve this in 3 simple steps:

1. Find companies with large databases full of unsold leads or previous buyers
2. Pitch them on using our AI Sales Android to convert those leads into SALES or get their previous buyers to buy more stuff
3. Install our Sales Android and run it

The tech behind each component is what may change as this industry matures and better tools come out.

The 3-step process to get companies results will not change because this service has been around for many years. What we're doing is called "database reactivation" (DBR). DBR is incredibly effective AND profitable when done right. The problem is it normally requires good salespeople to handle the work. This process takes a long time for humans because they have to reach out to each lead manually, and you're relying on people to follow a process.

However, with AI, we can now use it to reach out to old leads and "reactivate" them instead of labor-intensive (and expensive) salespeople.

Controlling Assets Vs. Owning Assets

There's another very important reason why this process is so effective. Not only for getting great results for companies, but also for building wealth for anyone who tries it.

When we look at the world's richest people, people like Elon Musk, Jeff Bezos, through to the older folks like John D. Rockefeller, Andrew Carnegie, and Henry Ford, how did they get rich?

It comes down to this simple formula:
Cash + Growth = Wealth

They first created a vehicle that produced cash flow, which allowed them to use that cash to acquire assets. The more they grew their cashflow vehicle, the more assets they purchased, and the more those assets rose in value, the wealthier they got. It gets to the point where your assets are growing so much that it pays for your day-to-day living. At that point, you're truly "free" because you no longer need to work yet can still take care of all your needs.

We can see this at a lower "wealth" level as well. Many average folks have slowly acquired real estate, building a property portfolio that then allowed them to become wealthy.

See how it is the acquisition of assets that makes one rich?

But there are 2 problems. First, creating a cash-flowing vehicle (likely a business) is not easy. *If* you manage to pull it off, it takes years of stress, sacrifice, and risk. You could do this via a 9-5, but again, this is very rare, and only the smartest, highest-paid people can successfully do it. Second, it takes a heck of a long time! Most of these millionaires and billionaires are in their 60s or 70s.

All of this means acquiring enough assets to make a difference to your net worth—while you're still young enough to enjoy it—is out of reach for most folks. So where does that leave those us who didn't graduate from Harvard and don't wanna wait 30 years to be well off?

That's where the beauty of ROYA comes in. Because there's nothing in the rulebook that says you have to OWN the assets to benefit from them!

In fact, what we can do instead is gain CONTROL of assets and, with a bit of magic, turn them into cash-flowing machines that pay us every week or month like clockwork. When we have enough cash coming in on autopilot to pay for all of our living costs and then some, we become financially free!

The real gold is how FAST we can do it. I can do this on my Facebook profile, send a couple of direct messages, and get control of a cash-flowing asset that has the potential to pay me $1k/week, possibly more, in an afternoon.

How many houses would you have to purchase to earn the same? How long might that take?

There's NOTHING like this, and that's why I'm so hyped to share this "30-year wealth shortcut" with you.

With that said, let's get back on track…

The Old Way Of Lead Generation

Every business works in roughly the same way. It doesn't matter what they sell, what niche they're in, which country, and so on. They all follow this sales process:

1. **Traffic:** Get eyeballs on their product/service
2. **Purchase:** Get them to buy something
3. **Upsell:** Get them to spend more money

The difference in the sales process largely depends on what product they're selling and the conversion process to get someone to make a purchase.

For example, if you are selling candles in an online store, the prospect would come onto the website and either purchase straight off the site or browse around and leave.

If you were selling something like life insurance, a lead would typically show intent by signing up for something or requesting a call. From there, a salesperson would close them over the phone.

Typically, it's higher priced products/services (say over $1,000) that require a face-to-face or higher-touch conversion process.

Our ROYA process works for both, but there's a reason why we prefer "high-ticket" products/services, which I'll discuss in **Part 4 – Getting ~~Clients~~ Partners**.

For the purpose of this discussion, let's assume we're talking about a solar company. A solar company sells solar panels for homes to save costs and energy. (Solar is an incredibly lucrative niche with high margins, and many of our students have crushed it here.)

Now, for decades the standard operating procedure for businesses when it comes to lead generation has been deeply flawed. Say this solar company spends money on advertising, trade shows, or other lead sources to build up a database of potential customers.

On the day those leads came in, the sales team would make calls and try to book appointments or make sales. If the prospect picked up and they bought something, great, done deal. If they didn't pick up, the salesperson might call a few times a day for the next 2-3 days. If the lead still didn't pick up or show any interest in having a call, they may be flagged as "dead leads" and never contacted again.

This is how many businesses end up with huge databases of 5,000, 10,000, or even 1,000,000+ contacts who have never bought anything despite having shown at least some level of interest, at some point.

If you were to pick 100 companies from a list of any industry and ask them what they're doing with their database of old leads, I bet you 9 times out of 10 they'd say a big fat *NOTHING*.

When I hear stuff like this, bells start ringing in my head, and I see dollar signs!

Check this out:

If we're talking about a solar company that might sell solar panel installations for $5,000 to $10,000 a pop... and it has a database of 50,000 contacts... even if you were to ONLY "revive" 1% and turn them into sales... that would be worth $2.5 million to $5 million in FOUND money!

And when you know how to lock in 50% revenue share deals by finding "hidden money" in people's businesses... this is when you make it rain and start getting paid big bucks.

But you might be thinking: if so much money is on the table... how come companies don't do this themselves? They simply don't have the time, skill, or knowledge.

Think about what a business owner has to do each day just to keep their business afloat: manage inventory, fulfill orders, deal with customer service issues, solve supplier problems, handle payroll and accounting, file taxes, ensure legal compliance, and more. They're stretched too thin already just running the day-to-day operations.

Re-engaging old leads at scale requires a specialized skill set, and it generally falls by the wayside as a "someday" project that never gets proper attention.

But that's where we come in. We have the expertise. We have the tools. We can take their database of leads they're not using and turn it into new sales. I can tell you now: no one is making an offer like this. Everyone's trying to get a cut of the NEW sales, and that's why competition is so hot. For us, when we switch the focus to "trash can" assets they don't care about, they're happy to offload them onto us. In their minds, they're thinking, "Have at it! I doubt you can make money off those dead leads, but if you can, great."

This usually means they have low expectations, so when we start turning their "dirt" into "gold," we blow their minds. That usually leads to, "What else can you help with?"

This is how we get our claws into a business, retain them for years, and become trusted partners.

Now, that's the business side of things.

Let's take a moment and discuss how ROYA is different from the traditional lead generation agency model (the same model I used when I started).

The Typical Ad Agency

There are a ton of different ways to do lead generation, but one of the most common strategies is going after NEW leads via Facebook (Meta) Ads. It's a great service. I did it for many years. But it has a huge flaw.

This flaw is the amount of work required to get the first win. And when you're working with a new company, your ability to get a "quick win" is going to determine if they keep working with you.

Assuming you've been able to land a client doing Facebook Ads, down below is a list of everything you need to get done before any SALES come in (sales are the most important thing for any biz owner—when they're spending money and no sales are coming in, they start getting very antsy).

- Get access to their Facebook Ad account (if they don't have one, you need to create a new page, populate it, and make it look "legit," set up the Facebook Ad account, the Facebook Pixel, and all that jazz)
- Research the market (if you don't know enough about them)
- Write the landing page copy

- Create the landing page and all the tech and systems behind it to ensure a lead comes through and is tagged properly
- Hook up the landing page to their customer relationship management system (CRM)
- Write the ad copy
- Create the ad creatives
- Create the ad campaigns
- Troubleshoot any issues that come up
- Launch the ads
- Monitor stats
- Fix any issues before burning through too much ad spend
- Fingers crossed that leads come in
- Fingers crossed that leads pass through to the sales team
- Wait for the sales team to take sales calls to ascertain the quality of leads
- If leads are crap, unqualified, not good, or too expensive, then figure out what's wrong, likely write new ads and new campaigns, and keep testing for another 1 or 2 months

If you've done this 10,000 times, it'll be easy for you. If it's your first time or even 10th time? You're going to pull your hair out. I don't know many more stressful activities than watching ad spend creep up each day from $50, $100, $500, $1,000 with minimal results to show, knowing once you blow too much of your client's money, that's your new gig gone.

There are so many moving parts. So much can go wrong at every stage.

If you don't mind complexity or taking on a huge amount of stress, maybe this is a good path for you to go down.

But if you don't want all the stress, this simple shift will make your life a LOT easier:

Instead of going after NEW leads, which means we have to shoulder all the RISK… we go after OLD leads to bring them back online and turn them into NEW sales in a couple of days.

The NEW Stress-Free Way To Do Lead Generation

Think about it. If someone has shown interest in a product or service, it means they've gone through a bit of your sales process, which means they know about the company and what you do. So would it make sense that this person is easier to close than someone who's never heard of you?

They definitely are, and that's why database reactivation, which we discussed before, is so effective.

In fact, we developed the Sleeping Beauty Android specifically to run database reactivation campaigns.

She's lovingly named Sleeping Beauty because she wakes up dead leads. Her weapon of choice is the Prince Charming SMS Kiss, a unique 2-sentence SMS we use to get 40-60% reply rates from dead leads.

Once you get your first database reactivation client, here's all you need to do:

1. Get the company to send you a batch of their old leads in a CSV spreadsheet file
2. Load them into a software called HighLevel
3. Install our Sleeping Beauty Android
4. Let our Android loose on those leads and wait for it to "chat" to the leads as they come in and book them into the sales team's calendars
5. Make $$

And the best part? All of this can happen within a week! Can you imagine signing a company and getting them SALES within a week? I'm not saying it'll be this fast each time, but even if it took 2 weeks, it's a lot faster and less risky than blowing $1,000 on ads and waiting 30-60 days with no guarantee of anything coming back.

Our Secret Weapon For Higher Booked Calls: SMS

The way people buy and respond to sales processes is changing. People don't like being cold-called anymore and rarely pick up unknown numbers. This makes it very difficult for companies who still rely on calling up leads to book sales calls.

This is why SMS is working so well for us. Instead of blowing up their phone at inconvenient times, we can send an SMS and get 40-50%+ reply rates. That's significantly better than the industry norm, which can be anywhere from 0-10%.

Here's one example from a PCP client of ours.

If you don't know, PCP stands for Personal Contract Purchase. These are loans provided to anyone who purchased a car on finance. Right now, there's a huge deal being made about people mis-sold on PCPs. Folks are able to claim back somewhere between $4,000 – $6,000 each if eligible.

Lawyers are running these campaigns, and they're trying to get ahold of anyone who had a PCP to run a check. If the claimant is successful, the solicitor can take a 30% cut of the total amount, which means anywhere between $1,200 – $1,800 in commission for them. These are usually done on a no-win-no-fee basis.

We partnered with a company that gave us a database of 935 leads to begin with. These leads had been dialed to death and were uncontactable.

So, our job was to reactivate them using our Sleeping Beauty Android and see if we could convert them into sales.

We have a number of "steps" in our lead process:

1. Lead Contacted
2. Lead Replied
3. Lead Qualified
4. DSAR Completed
5. Sent To Client

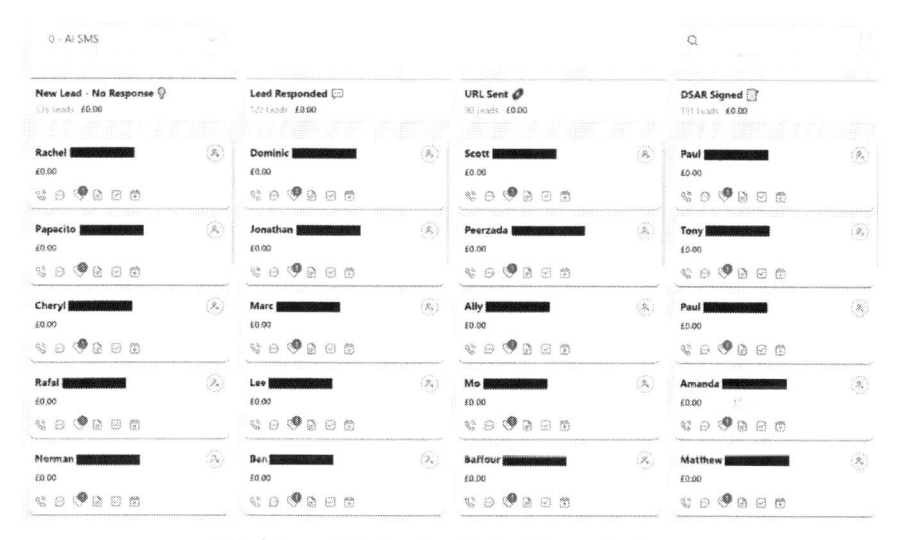

HighLevel "pipeline" dashboard view showing each step a lead goes through

This whole process is automated. Our Sleeping Beauty Android will send out the initial SMS; once the lead replies, it will ask a number of questions, overcome objections, and push towards getting the DSAR completed.

Here's an example of a conversation our Android had with a lead and successfully booked into a call:

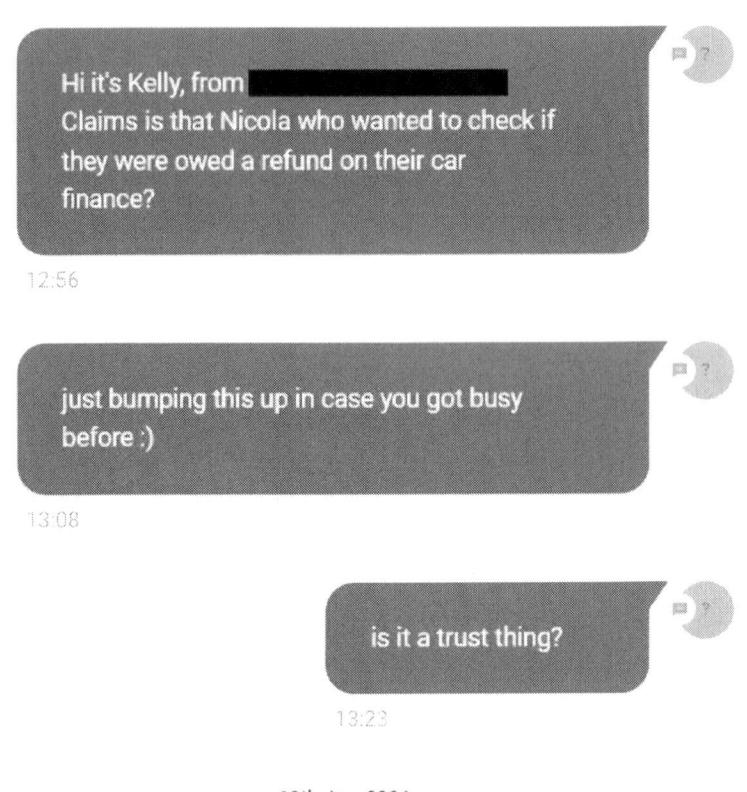

> Hi it's Kelly, from [redacted] Claims is that Nicola who wanted to check if they were owed a refund on their car finance?
>
> 12:56

> just bumping this up in case you got busy before :)
>
> 13:08

> is it a trust thing?
>
> 13:23

13th Jan, 2024

> Yes I would like to check. I had 2 cars on finance during 2013 to 2019.

> That's great, Nicola! Do you happen to have your vehicle finance agreement documents handy for those cars?

09:17

No sorry, not to hand

09:17

> No worries at all, Nicola. We can actually submit a Data Subject Access Request (DSAR) on your behalf to get those documents for you. Could you please complete this short DSAR form by clicking on this URL
>
> ▬▬▬▬▬▬▬▬▬▬▬▬▬▬▬▬▬▬▬
>
> hp'? It'll help us move things forward for you.

Dan Wardrope

> What is the process from here? Do you let me know if I am eligible to make a claim once you retrieve the docs and then I confirm I want to proceed?
>
> 09:20

Absolutely, Nicola. Once you've completed the DSAR form, we'll request your vehicle finance agreement and review it. If we find that you're eligible for a claim, we'll get in touch with you to discuss the next steps. It typically takes us about 30 working days to get everything sorted. Remember, we operate on a no-win no-fee basis, so there's no risk to you. Just pop over to the URL and fill out the form when you can:

hp'.

09:20

> Thanks.
>
> 09:20

It's pretty crazy that AI did all of this, right? It even handled an objection right there.

Now, this DSAR stands for "Data Subject Access Request." It allows the client to get information from the car companies. By doing this, they are confirming they are happy to move forward with the process towards getting a refund.

Here's what happened with this initial batch of 935 leads:

Reply rate = 42% (industry average is about 20%)

DSAR Signed rate = 20.4%

In real terms, it cost $21.04 to get someone to sign up and complete the sales process because it was all handled by AI, and no phone calls or salespeople were involved.

The solicitor can then collect $1,200 – $1,800 in fees per sale.

The return on investment is huge!

On top of this, our fee structure was $190 for every lead we got to DSAR stage.

That means for this small batch, we had 190 DSAR signed and invoiced the client for $36,100.

Not bad for a small project where AI did 90% of the work.

In the debt consolidation niche, we got ahold of a small batch of 319 leads. These were 3 days old and had been dialed 10 times each!

The sales team had given up, thinking they were deader than dead.

We fired up our Sleeping Beauty Android and were able to get 23% of those folks to book a call. That's not just getting in contact with them. That's from a dead lead to a hot, qualified lead. The business owner couldn't believe it!

Especially because each lead is worth $1,000 – $5,000.

At 73 red-hot leads back in the sales process, that's worth $73,000 to $365,000 in FOUND sales from a tiny list.

It's not unusual for us to get ahold of databases that are 10,000 up to the millions in numbers. That's where the real money's at.

If you're not already sold on why this is so powerful, here are a few more reasons why I think it's the best thing since sliced bread:

- We don't need fancy copywriting skills.
- We don't need to run any ads or have elite paid ads skills.
- We don't need to risk much; all we need to make this work is a laptop and internet.
- We get CONTROL of a database a company has spent $10,000s-plus, sometimes millions, building for us.
- The company takes zero risk yet has unlimited upside.
- We get paid for solving problems—and there's no limit to how much.
- We can run a million-dollar business with just one person.
- We focus on SYSTEMS, which means taking on more partners does not kill our profit margins or make us work harder.

I could go on!

Why ROYA Is The Strongest Offer In The Market

In marketing, we talk a lot about "making offers." An offer is nothing more than something that gets someone the outcome they want.

An offer can be as simple as, "Do you want a drink?" If the person is thirsty, they will say "yes." If they're not, they may say "no." That's why who you target is critical. If you want to get as many people to say "yes" as possible, go after thirsty people!

Knowing how to create powerful offers and pitch them determines any entrepreneur's success.

Now, I could write an entire book about how to craft offers, but for now, I'm just going to equip you with the basics.

To create irresistible offers that your ideal prospect can't say "no" to, my mentor, Travis Sago, uses the acronym TIMER.

TIMER stands for:

- **T**ime (how much time is required to do the thing?)
- **I**dentity (how does this match up with who I want to be?)
- **M**oney (how much will this cost me?)
- **E**nergy (how much effort do I need to put in?)
- **R**eputation (how will this make me look in front of my peers?)

In knowing this, we can determine the best offers that target a specific need for a specific person in a way that requires them to put in the least amount of *Time*, *Energy*, and *Money* while enhancing their *Identity* and *Reputation*.

In order for me to demonstrate why ROYA is so much better than anything else you can sell online, let's compare it using a little chart.

Imagine for a second that you're a new online service provider.

You've just heard about this "make money online" thing, and you are determined to get your first client.

You have a choice between providing 3 different online services to business owners.

Option 1. Copywriting: Your offer being, "I'll write you daily emails for $5k/month."

Option 2. Facebook Ads Agency: Your offer being, "I'll run your Facebook Ads for $3k/month."

Option 3. ROYA (AI Database Reactivation): Your offer being, "I'll reactivate your database and help you make more sales for a 50% cut."

Let's rate each of these "offers" out of 10, using the TIMER categories from the perspective of a client.

For example, a 10 on the scale for *Time* means a business owner doesn't need to waste any time with you because he can trust you to get on with the job.

A 10 on the *Money* scale means this is super affordable to them. A 1 means it's super expensive and makes it harder to make a decision to work with you.

A 10/10 on everything is essentially: "Hell yes, I want to work with you!"

A 1/10 on everything is essentially: "Hell no, I wouldn't touch you with a 10-foot pole."

Make sense? As a business owner being pitched these 3 services, here's where I think they sit:

	Copywriting: I'll write you daily emails for $5k/month	Facebook Ads Agency: I'll run your Facebook Ads for $3k/month	ROYA: I'll reactivate your database and help you make more sales for a 50% cut
Time	3	3	10
Identity	3	3	8
Money	1	1	10
Energy	8	8	10
Reputation	3	4	9
TOTAL	18	19	47

Why am I rating copywriting and Facebook Ads services so low?

From an offer creation side, the simple fact that a company has to pay for a service before getting the result throws in a lot of objections to saying yes.

In order for them to hand over a chunk of change, they subconsciously weigh up the deal through the TIMER lens.

If you're a newbie and they know your skills aren't as fleshed out, they know they have to handhold you more. If you mess up, they have to take that into account. If you mess up really bad, it could affect their reputation. All of this takes energy away from them. Once you stack enough of these negative points, the deal becomes hard to say "yes" to for them.

However, there's one more thing.

Behind the TIMER currencies that a biz owner needs, they also need certainty. The more certainty you can provide to them, the easier it is for them to agree to work with you. It's hard to pitch a $5k/month copywriting retainer to a client as a newbie because they don't know if you'll make them back the $5k. They may end up losing the $5k AND 10+ hours of working with you.

On the other hand, if you sell ROYA, a system that produces a result, the results aren't based on a human's limited skills, knowledge, and experience, but on the system's reliability. In order to demonstrate a system's reliability, all you need to do is demonstrate it works. Once a biz owner can see it working and can solve his problem, the sale is done. Certainty is high.

On top of this, we juice up the offer even more by saying we'll do this for the business owner and the business only pays us after we make sales. This final nail in the coffin removes the money obstacle, and that's why our offer is so deadly. We do ALL the work. The SYSTEM gets the results, reliably and consistently, and we only get paid AFTER it works. Every single objection is removed.

It goes a little further! Right now our economy's in a bad place. Companies are facing increased cost of goods and services and lower revenues. This means their profit margins are being squeezed. We discussed this in the previous part.

What we're offering them isn't just a low-risk system that produces results. It's a system that both increases revenue while decreasing costs at the same time. If AI can replace one or two of your salespeople and save you $100k/year while adding a couple million to your bottom line, it becomes a no-brainer.

Dan Wardrope

How David Went From A Struggling Lead Gen Agency To Working With The UK's Top Solar Agency

David fell into lead generation by mistake. He was a software engineer, selling websites on the side. After he delivered a fresh website one day, the client asked him, "Will this get me leads as well?"

David said, "Not really. To get more leads, you'll need to run ads."

He didn't know anything about ads at the time, but after that client offered to pay him $600 to do it, he became a lead genner overnight.

In the years that followed, David got more and more into paid ads lead generation, working with mostly smaller companies. The problem is, he never really "made it."

And the main reason for that is because he struggled to get clients and retain the clients he did get.

When selling lead generation, he was competing against every other agency. As soon as he pitched his services, he'd be ghosted or sent a typical canned response, "We already have leads and suppliers. What makes you different?"

And the truth is, there isn't really any difference between one agency versus another, and so it would inevitably come down to price, ending up as a race to the bottom.

He also found the churn rate incredibly high. Because he was working with a lot of smaller companies, they didn't have very good sales processes in place. This meant whenever his leads came in, and for some reason, either the main sales guy was sick, on holiday, lazy, or not in the mood, his leads wouldn't get dialed. As a result, he'd get blamed for the poor lead quality. The result? He'd get fired.

Then David found the ROYA system and immediately knew this would solve every problem he had. Fast forward a year, he's now working with one of the biggest Solar agencies in the UK, is fully booked out, able to easily close clients, get referrals, and his retention rate is better than anything he's ever experienced. He's doing so well that I brought him on as a vetted "Tech Terminator," someone who builds Sales Androids for students in my community!

Dan Wardrope

Why Everyone Selling AI Is Going To Fail

AI is huge right now, and whenever there's a trendy new thing, it creates a buying frenzy. So, it's no surprise people are trying to find ways to cash in on this.

But everyone's going about it the wrong way, and that's why I think 99% of these guys will fail (just like 99% of the folks who went panning for gold in the California Gold Rush of 1884).

Just look around the market right now, and you'll see a ton of people either trying to create their own AI businesses, hooking up ChatGPT API to some semi-fancy interface, building an AI app, or turning their copywriting agency into an AI copy agency that churns out 1000s of mediocre copy in just 24 hours.

Most of these new AI apps and businesses will be obsolete in a few months. The big boys (like ChatGPT and Claude) can start and launch the same features quicker than them, and because their audience is so much bigger, they'll get traction and eat these guys alive.

The guys branding themselves as AI copy agencies... well, they've just turned their high-touch agency into a commodity that can be easily replaced.

And the last kind are the "get-rich-quick" boys and girls trying to sell $97/month software-as-a-service subscriptions (SaaS). That's fine until they realize they need 100 new customers every month just to make $9,700 per month and an extra 50 customers to refill the ones that drop out the month before. This model is completely unsustainable unless you have deep pockets to keep acquiring new customers.

If you're intent on doing life and providing for your family in "hard mode," that's totally cool. But maybe you're a bit more like me and want to do it as much on "easy mode" as possible? Then check out Rob's story…

Story Time: How A 9-5er Quit His Job And Is On Track To Do 8-Figures PROFIT In His First Year

$10 million dollars. That's how much 8 figures is.

Here's a story of one of my top students, Rob Brown.

Rob has been killing it since implementing the ROYA system, so much so that I'm constantly amazed at how fast he's making progress.

See, Rob came from a sales background. He'd spent 20 years working for "the man" and was doing okay, taking home a modest ~$72k a year. But he wasn't satisfied and knew there was no way he'd get rich going down the path he was on.

Rob and I were acquaintances since he had bought leads from me over the years. One day, he caught wind of what I was doing with AI and felt like this could be his ticket out of the 9-5 grind.

The only problem? He had zero tech skills and was afraid he couldn't make it work. That didn't stop him because he could see how this little system could totally disrupt the industry and solve all the problems he'd been dealing with managing sales teams.

And he was right! After phoning around and taking his first few "coffee dates" (what we call sales meetings in our world) and demoing the ROYA system over Zoom, he started to see everyone's eyes light up at what this could do for them.

In his FIRST week, he signed 2 companies.

In his mind, if he could make $12k/month, he'd be able to quit his job and be comfortable. It didn't take him long to figure out that he could make a LOT more than that.

Rob cracked on building Sales Androids for these companies while continuing to have coffee date after coffee date. I can't emphasize how important this point is. Your BIGGEST priority that will make or break your success in this game is focusing on the number of coffee dates. You want as many meetings as you can get. Stack 'em up first, then worry about fulfillment and picking the right partners later.

If you overthink this part, you'll stall and never get started. I always teach my students to "build the parachute on the way down!"

Rob embodies this, and that's why he gained traction so quickly. In fact, he saw the potential so much that he wanted to create more time to work on this. That's when he handed in his notice and went "all in" just 2 weeks into trying out ROYA and BEFORE any money had come in yet! Talk about ballsy.

His gamble paid off because just a few weeks after leaving his 9-5, he received his first $25k in PROFIT.

Let me put this into perspective. Rob heard about me in late December 2023. He joined me inside my ROYA program on January 8th, 2024. He quit his job on January 29th, 2024.

4 weeks later, in early March 2024, he was already making $25k/month.

But things are just getting started.

People started hearing about what he was doing. With a little extra referral incentive, droves of potential clients started tapping on his door. Not just any clients but mammoth household brand names that everyone knows.

These guys had entire teams of AI specialists trying to work out how to do what Rob was doing and they couldn't figure it out! They were pulling their hair out and left with no choice but to hire Rob to do it.

Later that same month, March 2024, Rob updated me and told me he was doing crazy numbers with one class action lawsuit client. Because of the nature of their business and their deadlines coming up, they urgently need leads in the door ASAP, to the degree they're willing to pay Rob upfront. How much? $100k per WEEK. This would soon double to $200k per week to have him target more and more leads. Remember, this is just one client. Rob has many, and his pipeline is full.

He started from scratch in early January 2024 and, by April 2024, is on track to smash sales records of companies that have been around for YEARS. I think he might be the fastest company in the UK to hit 8 figures in his first year of trading.

Better yet, because Rob's mostly a one-man band so almost all of that is pure profit.

But Rob isn't the only one getting incredible results.

Here are a few more...

Gary
Mar 27 (edited) • ROYA Wins

1st customer launched finally!

25 leads contacted
1 sale
3 more sales appointments booked
5 other active conversations going on

all in the first 3 hours! holy moly!

Thankyou so so much to @Aaron Rowley for helping me set this up and all the dumb questions he had to persevere with from my end ;) you are a champion mate ty!

Gary launched his Sales Android to a tiny list
of 25 contacts and got a sale in just 3 hours.

Jack ▮
Mar 22 · ROYA Wins

£10k/m and 8 new clients in 30 days! (Just by DM'ing a few people a Day)

It finally happened, two consecutive months at £10k! I wanted to thank Dan, I've tried everything from Dropshipping to SMMA, to affiliate marketing, and I can't believe how easy this has been to sell.

Bare with me, I'm not a copywriter and definitely not a salesman, but somehow I still did it.

And for full transparency, I joined ROYA In December but sat on going through Dan's training for way to long!

I've not done any ads; I just sent 30 messages a day on LinkedIn with some automation software, and I was getting a decent amount of calls a week.

I'm not a salesman, but I still managed to close at around 60%. And of the people I didn't close, 30% didn't have a list, and 10% I didn't want to work with.

> *Having tried every Make Money Online model, Jack tried ROYA and is crushing it while regularly hitting £10k (~$13k) months.*

> I have had someone offer me £150K for 5% equity, but I was trying to avoid it

One student got offered £150k ($190k) for just 5% equity in his AI Automation Agency. That values his 2-month-old company at £3m ($3.8m)!

Kevan
Mar 1 (edited) · ROYA Wins

$5K/Month Property Education Client

Guys, I just walked out of a meeting with a new Property Education client. $5K per month retainer, Costs covered + $25 per booked appointment and 100K list. F@ck Yes...

Kevan closes a modest $5k/month plus performance-based compensation client in the Property Education space.

Dan Wardrope

FB Ads Success!

Congrats @Trevor

$226 in ad spend at $20 per day - as per the training
4 demos done
Two last Friday, one today and one on Thursday. Partnership Agreements sent to all of them.

Today's call apparently, was for a solar salesman that works in a network with several installers that provide him leads to sell.

He is keen on getting started for himself and then partnering on becoming an enterprise vendor within the network of 5000 installers across 19 states!!

Trevor runs Facebook Ads and is on track to close 4 new partners.

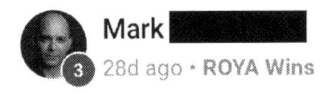

Mark
28d ago • ROYA Wins

Hoozah.. Sold my first AI robot

..Just got off my coffee date with an implant dentist. $497 + $497 mo for DBR on dead leads and unfinished dental treatment quotes.

I was getting nervous because I ruined a doctor lead yesterday with tech glitches trying to share my screen...But today went swimmingly.

Mark closes a hybrid deal at $497 upfront plus $497 per month.

Bernard
Apr 16 · ROYA Wins

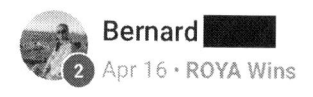

Just inked my first deal!

Just bought the ROYA program on Friday and today I got my first deal signed. It's for a real estate company that has 35k leads and several agents selling. Didn't go for commission since real estate is such a slow sales process. Settled for $60 per booked call.

This guy also has a mortgage brokerage company with about 5X as many leads but wanted to test it with real estate first.

Got two more coffee dates booked for later this week. Let's go!!

Bernard landed his FIRST deal a few days into our training.

Kevin
Apr 18 · ROYA Wins

100% WIN RATE - 2 FOR 2

It took me a little bit to get everything set up. I'm the kind of guy that wants to know what I'm talking about before reaching out to folks.

I pitched one person over text today and another on the phone and they are in! One of them hasn't even seen it but wants in 🙌 God is good!

Kevin's on track for a 100% close rate!

Dan Wardrope

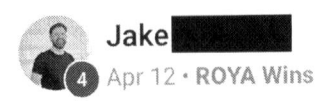

Jake
Apr 12 · ROYA Wins

First android went live and booked a call in 2 minutes!

I imported 5 contacts to test the drip mode, didn't even have time to open the conversation window and someone was already talking to Sarah and booking a call lol!

80 contacts sent, 29 responded, 7 calls booked in the first day with 2 more likely all from a 2 year old list.

$120 per call and I get 20% of profit on any deals on the backend in the property investment space.

That's the most I've ever made in 1 day on the very first day going live!

I worked really hard on this, pulling all nighters, zaps and workflows coming out of my ears, I've been trying to get off the ground in the online marketing world since 2016, before that I was in construction, and I had to go back to construction work last year to survive. I was very close to having to do that again but after going live yesterday with these results, I really think I'm going to make it now!

Thanks so much to everyone in the community especially @Dan Wardrope, @Graham Connolly, y and @ thanks for your help and support. You

Jake makes $940 PROFIT on his first go.

How A One-Man Agency From Antibes, France, Closes $22 Billion Dollar Companies

We have wins out the wazoo, but let me close Part 3 out with the story of Cedric Seguela.

Cedric runs a tiny little agency from Antibes, France. He isn't well known. He's not the most experienced in our community. He would not call himself the best of the best. Yet he regularly closes HUGE whale partners; we're talking some of the biggest in their space. Billion-dollar companies are vying for his attention.

Now, if Cedric was trying to sell Facebook Ads, there is no chance in hell he'd EVER get in the door with a billion-dollar company. They would never entertain his calls, let alone agree to deals where they're giving him up to 50% of the profits. This is unheard of!

Cedric regularly sends me updates on his exploits and they go a little like:

"That's NINE whale clients I've signed now!!"

"I've just secured a deal with an insurance firm with 25,000 employees."

"They're going to do 8k – 12k of leads per month and will pay me 2€ ($2.18) for each conversation."

> **Cedric Seguela**   1:17pm
> They have 25000 employees, the branch I am dealing with are handling approx 8000 to 12000 leads per months, and I am charging a flat fee for the set-up + 2€ for each convo, they cover all costs.

"Call complete with one of the largest solar companies in France."

> **Cedric Seguela**   1:08pm
> Hey Dan, I hope you are well. I had that call with the french solar whale that are doing 150M€/year. They are in the hundreds of thousand leads, they buy some from everyone and co, and they have 8 persons on staff to generate their own. Anyway, they are very keen,

"Another one!!! A home services group with 8 major construction brands."

> **Cedric Seguela**   2:48pm
> Another one !!! Meeting with the largest house builder in France, 8 brands. With the inflation and the house credit crunch, the last thing they want is more expensive leads. They want to maximize what they already got.

I've been selling lead gen services for nearly 10 years.

And I can tell you right now. This is NOT normal!

However, after seeing so many people with zero online experience and zero AI experience who are not Harvard graduates and do not have any special skills crushing it and landing huge deals, I'm starting to realize this IS normal. All it takes is knowing how to create great offers, put it in front of the right people, and show them how your system works. If it solves their problem in a unique way that no one else can do, you can command fees no one else can.

This is how newbies are landing 7-, 8- and 9-figure companies and completely turning around their lives and their family's lives. It's not about their skills, knowledge, or experience but everything about the SYSTEM that gets the result and their own resourcefulness to get down and do the work.

I hope you're starting to get just how incredible this opportunity is.

I don't know how long this will last. We have the entire world's economy to go after, so I'm sure it will be hard to saturate! But the early bird always gets the worm, especially when tech moves this fast. If you're on board, keep reading the next chapters where I'll show you how to get started right now.

How The ROYA System Works

Here's where the rubber meets the road. I'm going to give you a high-level overview. This will include some technical lingo because I can't avoid it. I'm not going to give you the technical instructions yet, because 1) I don't want to overwhelm you, and 2) I don't want to scare you off from trying this out.

The key to making this work is not worrying about the small details. Do not worry about understanding everything right away! To help you "get it," I've also linked video walk-throughs to explain, in case you're a visual learner or like to review the material a few times so it sinks in.

However, remember what I said before. Your TOP priority and focus should be on getting coffee dates/sales meetings with potential prospects. Everything else can be figured out along the way. If you understand even a little about tech, it should take a few days to "get it" and then a few more to make it work. Rob Brown, who's on track to do $10m+ in his first year, also did not know any of this when he started. If he can do it, and if I can do it, you can too!

The Process

Remember earlier I told you that this is what we do:

Every business has dead leads sitting in its database. Leads the businesses spent good money on and will never get back. This is costing the industry BILLIONS in lost sales.

With our AI Sales Android, we turn your dead leads into new SALES automatically—without any upfront costs, even if they've been dialed to death by your sales team already.

Here's EXACTLY how we make it happen:

Step 1: The Approach

We approach business owners and ask them if they have any old leads.

If they do have old leads, we ask them if they want us to turn them into sales using SMS and AI.

If they say "yes," we propose (up to) a 50% profit share on any sale we make from those old leads.

What do you think we say if they say, "NO WAY DUDE, THAT'S TOO MUCH!"?

Do you think we barter, beg, or bargain to avoid yet more rejection? NOPE!

We say, "Would you prefer 100% of NOTHING, or 50% of $100k?"

This is when the penny drops. They then ask, "How does it work? Can we see a demo?"

Step 2: The Coffee Date

Once they've confirmed interest in our pitch, we set up a Zoom call.

We call it a COFFEE DATE.

We prepare for the coffee date by copying and pasting a simple prompt template into the OpenAI playground. (I'll show you how to do this later; it's pretty neat.)

We run through the DEMO on the coffee date by screen sharing over Zoom without having to build anything or having any AI skills at all. (Again, we'll show you how later.)

Step 3: The Close

Finally, we close the company, agree on the financials, and send our contracts over.

What do you guys think the close rate is?

Close to 100%—even if you don't have any experience or case studies.

Why? Because you've just shown them on screen what this system can do. As soon as they see it in action, they're sold.

Step 4: The Sleeping Beauty Android Build

Once everything is signed, we request a CSV file of their old leads.

We load them into a super easy-to-use CRM called High-Level. HighLevel is where we send SMSs and track our leads in the sales process.

This is also where our AI bot lives. In this instance, we call her our Sleeping Beauty Android. She's configured to know how to "speak" to leads in a particular niche, ask questions, qualify them, overcome objections, and then book them into sales calls.

Step 5: The Prince Charming Kiss

You can't have a Sleeping Beauty without a Prince Charming. So when we fire up our Sleeping Beauty Android, her first message sent to the lead is using what we call a "Prince Charming Kiss." This is designed to "wake up" dead leads and turn them into qualified sales calls.

Step 6: The Sales Call

Once the lead is qualified by our Sleeping Beauty Android, it will book them into the client's calendar for the sales team to dial.

Step 7: Profit

If the lead makes a purchase, we collect our cut of the profits.

Step 8: Repeat

After that, we just rinse and repeat: hitting more leads, reactivating more people, and making more sales.

Make sense so far?

Prefer to watch a video explanation of this? Scan the QR code or head over to:
https://link.flexxable.com/overview

Part 4
Getting ~~Clients~~ Partners

Now it's time to get into the good stuff! First, let's make the distinction between "clients" versus "partners."

I've used the term "clients" a lot in this book so far, mainly because it's easily understood by most people. However, I never call the people I work with clients, and after I explain this to you, you shouldn't either.

What does it mean when you have a client? What does it feel like? It feels like a lot of responsibility, and it feels like that person, in some ways, "owns" you. Not in the literal sense, but a client pays you to get a job done. But we don't do jobs. We solve problems. And when we solve problems, we deserve to be paid well for it. Most client businesses are nothing more than having 10 bosses who all demand their pound of flesh and are more interested in you clocking in the hours than in your results.

In addition to this, a client doesn't see you as equal. You are an expense item on their balance sheet and that means you are an employee to them. An employee doesn't get a share of the profits. This is why we want to get away from this when seeking the ability to negotiate revenue share deals.

For all these reasons, we call our clients PARTNERS instead. As partners, we are of equal standing. We share the risk if it goes belly up, and we share in the profits when we win!

Okay, now let's move on…

When getting into this game, one of the first things everyone asks me is, "Which niche should I go after?"

I get it. You don't want to make a mistake and be saddled with a dud niche. You also want to pick one that has an outsized payoff. I mean, why go after a small niche and make less money when you can go after a bigger one and make more?

So, in this chapter, I'm going to break down not just which partners I think you should go after, but how to get in front of them, how to pitch the ROYA system, and how to close them.

Let's begin…

Who ROYA Works For (And Best Niches)

Having worked this system and directly coached over 400+ students, along with thousands more indirectly, I now know that you should **not** pick a niche.

Yes, that might fly in the face of every guru who says you should "niche down." But here's my reasoning: the only reason to pick a niche is to make it easier for you to get good partners and "stand out" from your competitors.

However, when you sell a system like ROYA that solves a business problem that everyone has, and everyone wants, it means you don't need to "stand out" and pigeonhole yourself into one niche. You can go to anyone and everyone. This allows you to maximize opportunities and choose your best partners.

Some of my most successful students, like Rob and Cedric, do this, and they're landing big fish every week in all kinds of different industries.

These range from anything like solar, roofing, mortgage, life insurance, credit repair, debt finance, car finance, personal injury, class action, dog training, beauty salon, cosmetic surgery, dental, mis-sold claims…

Basically, with the ROYA system, any industry that requires a salesperson to chase leads and close them are great potential partners.

As a rule of thumb here are the criteria for what I consider a good partner to work with:

- They sell a product/service with a high margin.
- They sell something over $1,000 (unless they're e-Commerce and can do high volume).
- They are already advertising and bringing in fresh leads.
- They are chill to work with and want everyone to win.
- They have a database of at least 1,000 contacts.
- They are good at closing (30% close rate minimum).

You will only find out some of this after speaking with them during your coffee date, but this will give you a head start. Remember, don't bother about niching down. Just speak to anyone and everyone with a sales team and pitch this service!

You can also get creative with this. Because this is a sales process, it can be used in alternative areas like e-Commerce, online coaching, info products, and more. You just need to figure out how to do it and work the prompts to fit the niche.

E-Commerce is interesting because you're usually working with very large databases. The margins per sale are lower but when you can work in high volume, that can more than make up for it. For example, I negotiated a $50 commission per sale of a testosterone supplement. Their database is in the hundreds of thousands. If I convert just 1% of 100,000 contacts, that's worth $500,000!

There are thousands of e-Commerce stores with big databases out there, and they're not doing much with them. This is a golden opportunity for us.

Selling Principles For Maximum Sales

Right now, we're getting incredible "close rates." If you don't know what that means, it's essentially the percentage of deals closed. If I took 10 calls and closed 3 of them, that would be a 30% close rate. A 30% close rate in any industry is generally pretty solid.

The unusual thing about ROYA is that we're able to get at least 60%+ close rates, sometimes 100%. Many of the people selling are doing it on their FIRST go, which means they don't have experience selling anything and certainly do not have experience selling a brand-new system they barely understand.

This is absolutely bonkers.

Imagine having 10 calls and coming away with 10 deals. This is the reality right now because the system solves a burning need. All we do is put our ROYA offer in front of the people who need it, and once they see how it works, they want it. No need for high-pressure tactics. No need for fancy sales skills. No need to "defuse objections."

There are, however, a few selling principles that we abide by that will help you 1) get more coffee dates and 2) close more deals.

Let's get into it…

Selling Principle 1: Widen The Yes Hole

When trying to sell anything, one of the biggest objections is price. The higher the price, the bigger the commitment and the more the logical mind needs to justify the purchase.

If you're trying to sell a $5k/month lead gen service to a biz owner, naturally, they will want to know if the money is being spent well. The only way to make business owners more likely to say "yes" is to provide proof and evidence of your successes. Once they see enough to make them feel comfortable with the purchase, then they commit.

The problem is if you do not have proof and evidence of success, trying to justify why a biz owner should hire you becomes much harder.

So, how do you get around this? You can lower your price. But if you do that, you become a commodity and the biz owner will think you're cheap because you're not very good. You make it easier to say "yes," but it also subtly conveys your low value.

We don't want to do that. That's why we do something wildly different than everyone else. We completely remove the price from the discussion by offering a 100% performance model.

By saying they pay ZERO upfront and only pay us after we make a sale for them, you are saying, *"Hey, Mr. Client, I back myself, and I'm willing to share the risk with you. If I make sales, we both win. If I don't make sales, we both take the hit."* Business owners are entrepreneurs at heart, which means they LOVE it when the people they work with are happy to get in the trenches with them and put their money where their mouth is.

This simple method massively widens the "yes hole." It makes it easy for anyone to agree to work with us. Because the upside is massive and the downside is minimal.

That said, if there's no exchange of money, some business owners will not be invested in the project because they don't have any "skin in the game." Not everyone is like this, but it can happen.

If you find yourself in this situation, we use a second principle called:

Selling Principle 2: Be Ready To Walk Away

We must always be ready to walk away from a bad deal. There are plenty more fish in the sea. A bad deal can be anything from numbers that don't make financial sense for you (perhaps they want to negotiate your 50% cut down to 25%. I know what I'm worth, so I will politely decline), the business owner is an a-hole and difficult to work with, or the company is slow providing the information you need to install the Sales Androids, delaying the time until you can make sales and get paid. There are an infinite number of bad deals besides these, and you need to know when to walk away.

The Instant AI Agency

I signed a deal with a great company not too long ago. It is an e-Commerce brand that sells candles. We had agreed to a $50 commission per sale. With their huge database, I knew we could all walk away with a good chunk of change. The problem is, as soon as my tech guy requested all the data and information we needed, they went radio silent.

Now, I don't make money unless we make sales. Any delay takes away from my ability to do that. So, I knew I had to get creative and (politely) show him my position. If he's changed his mind and doesn't want to do this anymore, I'm totally cool. Just let me know if it's a yes or no!

So here's what I sent:

Hi NAME,

The bot is built, ready, and waiting.

Your number has been approved for A2P, for sending SMS.

My prediction is we will convert 2-5% of your 100k buyers into additional sales.

That's 2k – 5k new orders.

> *I don't remember what your average order value is, but it's over $100, right?*
>
> *We are covering the SMS costs.*
>
> *We are covering the OpenAI costs.*
>
> *My team has already spent a week building this.*
>
> *We can be up and running in days.*
>
> *There is literally no downside for you guys.*
>
> *It's just found money.*
>
> *Unless there is something I am missing?*
>
> *Please just let me know because <u>my self-esteem is taking a beating right now</u>! ;)*
>
> *Dan*

I think the key bit that might save me here is highlighted and underlined above. I am appealing to their "good nature." And maybe making them feel a tad guilty, too.

A few minutes later, the business owner responded and confirmed that he was pushing to get this launched ASAP!

Don't be afraid to stay firm. We hold the keys. They need us more than we need them. What we have can save their business and make them fabulously wealthy. If they don't see that, that's on them! Plenty more fish in the sea.

And that leads us to the next selling principle:

Selling Principle 3: We Are The Prize

Or, as my mentor says, "We're the prettiest girl at the bar." This concept is super simple.

All you need to do is hold this frame of mind in your head as you enter the field. There's no need to be brash or overly confident if you don't want to, but know your worth! We are the prize. People want us because of what we can do, and that allows us to command the fees that we do.

If they could do what we could do, they would have done it already. The fact is, no one knows how to do it, and I've spoken to billion-dollar companies with entire AI teams who haven't cracked what we do yet. That's insane!

So do not let anyone bully you or make you take a deal that doesn't work for you, or you do not like.

Selling Principle 4: It's A HELL YES Or A HELL NO

This one's pretty simple. Whenever we're unsure whether to do a deal or not, we go back to this principle here.

It's either a HELL YES or a HELL NO.

This simply means if we're not all in on the deal and excited about it, do not do the deal. Just walk away; there are plenty more deals out there.

Do not feel the need to take on a bad deal or one you're uncomfortable with. Losing 1 to 3 months of time will hurt you more than just saying "no" and looking for the next one.

I use this same principle for anyone who wants me to coach them. If they're not all in, it's a no for both of us.

Selling Principle 5: Show, Don't Tell

The last selling principle I want to cover here is maybe the most important of all. It is the "show, don't tell" concept. If you know anything about copywriting, this is a core principle in writing good copy. This boils down to the fact that it is easier to convey an idea to someone when you show them, as opposed to telling them.

For example, let's say I have an image in my head right now. It is a long, smooth, brown tube-like shape wrapped around a soft white textured outer layer. Can you guess what it is? It's a hot dog!

Or I could just show you the image below instead, and you would get it instantly!

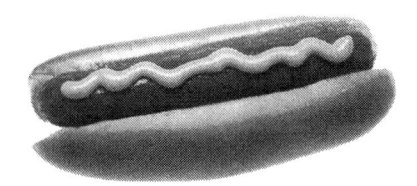

Based on this principle, the most effective way to sell the ROYA system is by SHOWING them. The way we do this is through a live demo of the system in action. We do this by screen sharing over Zoom. Once they see it working and taking a fake prospect through the sales process, answering their questions, and gently leading them into booking a call faster and more effectively than any salesperson can, we have them on the hook, and we've got the deal.

It's as easy as that, and you do not need any special sales skills. Just Zoom and a little inexpensive program called OpenAI.

The 4-Step Partner-Getting Process

While the ROYA system seems almost unbelievable at first, we've developed a simple 4-step process to get new partners on board seamlessly. This cuts through any objections or skepticism by demonstrating the power of AI upfront. By the end, they're chomping at the bit to get started.

Step 1: The Pitch

The initial offer is straightforward yet to the point: "Would you like us to turn your old leads into new SALES using our ChatGPT Sales Android?"

We lay it out very simply. They provide their database of dead leads/old customers, and we'll reactivate them into new sales using advanced AI messaging with no upfront costs and no risk. We only get paid a performance cut of any revenue we generate from reactivating their old data.

This offer is designed to stop them in their tracks. By proposing to monetize an asset they had completely written off, while taking on all the work and risk, we eliminate every objection. The sheer boldness and lack of risk make it a "no brainer."

Now, here's where a lot of folks mess up and the result is killing any opportunity of getting on a coffee date with a prospect.

Do not go in for the kill too early!

Do not talk about financials, percentage splits, or offering trial runs. Avoid any language that says, "Hey, I wanna sell you something!" This pushes people away, ESPECIALLY if they just met you.

As a rule of thumb, the "frame" you want to have for this part of the sales process is to imagine you're at a BBQ with the prospect you're talking to.

Your only goal is to tease them and get them excited to learn more.

I had a gentleman say he was struggling to book coffee dates and wanted me to review his pitch.

Here is his pitch:

> "Hey, since you've been in business for a while, do you have a pile of old dead landscaping leads? I can revive some of them using AI and turn this into new found revenue for you. We split the net profits 70/30 (better than you keeping 100% of nothing with those leads just gathering dust, and your overworked staff not able to tend to them properly). What do you think… open to a small trial run?"

Can you imagine how this went down? He got a lot of "no thanks" responses.

Instead, I advised him to change his strategy and loosen up!

Here is what I said he could try:

> "Dude, that landscaping job you did at the house on George Street was incredible. I can't believe the size of their pool; you must have wanted to dive in!
>
> "I was wondering if you have any old leads I can turn into George Street type jobs for you using ChatGPT on a backend deal?"

The first line is personalized (you will want to adjust this based on who you speak to). It creates a connection. The second line is a soft ask. We've found "backend" works well, but feel free to test.

THEN you move to a coffee date and show 'em how it works.

THEN talk financials.

Yes, it means you have to be a real person and cannot copy-paste the same message to 10,000 prospects.

But I promise you will get better results with a SNIPER approach rather than a machine gun approach.

Step 2: The Coffee Date

As I've mentioned, we call all our sales meetings "coffee dates." We don't like stuffy sales calls because our main goal of this meeting is to have a chat and see if we're a good fit and if we can do business together! If we can't have a relaxed conversation, and I think working together will be like pulling my nails out, it's a "no."

After we make a pitch, our only goal is to get them onto a coffee date. This is where we do all the discussions about HOW we reactivate leads, the financials, and so on.

I can get these done in 30 minutes. You don't need longer, but it might take a bit more for your first go.

Step 3: The Demo

This happens during your coffee date. After piquing their interest with our offer, it's time to demonstrate the ROYA system's capabilities. The EASIEST way to do this is just getting them on Zoom and, while screen sharing, walk them through our Sales Android in action.

To be clear, we do not build a full Sales Android here!

All we are doing is using OpenAI's Playground interface on their website to build our "demo."

OpenAI allows us to insert a pre-built prompt into the system and interact with it in real time.

Imagine when a partner is looking at their screen and seeing AI communicate naturally and effortlessly with a lead and handle any objections without any human intervention.

We want them to watch it and begin thinking, "If this can reactivate even 1% of my database, it'll be gold!"

Here's how it works:

1. Create an OpenAI account here: https://openai.com
2. Add $20 worth of credit (each message costs a small amount of $ to run).
3. Go to the Playground: https://platform.openai.com/playground
4. Create an Assistant and give it a name.
5. Choose the latest ChatGPT model (right now, GPT-4 is out, but choose whichever one is the latest version).
6. Insert a prompt into the "Instructions" section (see below).

Prompt Instructions

This is how we tailor our Android based on its niche. Below I'll give you one prompt for the life insurance niche and one custom prompt where you can fill in your own details as you wish.

Life Insurance Prompt, Example

Your job is to qualify leads over SMS for life insurance services. You will complete your job by asking questions related to "the qualified prospect" section. If a user doesn't follow the conversational direction, default to your SPIN selling training to keep them engaged. Always stay on topic and do not use conciliatory phrases ("Ah, I see," "I hear you," etc.) when the user expresses disinterest.

###

Your Output Style: casual message, conversational, US Idiom, American dialect

###

Your Training: The Challenger Sale, Life Insurance

###

FIRST Message: "It's Sarah from Flexxable Insurance here. Is this the same Dan who got a life insurance quote from us in the last couple of months?"

###

Qualified Prospect Section:

- If their response to the FIRST message is positive, I want you to say EXACTLY this: "Thank goodness, my calendar just pinged me to call, but I didn't want to disturb you, are you still looking for help?" But if their response to the FIRST message was negative, I want you to say EXACTLY this: "Sorry about that, just to confirm, are you interested in getting any life insurance?" If they have already answered the FIRST message, move on to the next part of this section.

- Ask them if there is anything important they'd like their policy to do or cover.

- Tell them we can help them and will beat any market price, then ask them if they'd like to schedule a callback

- If they say "yes," send the following message: "Great! Here's my calendar for you to book in a time: https://YOURCALENDARLINK.COM"

Rules:

- Only ask one question at a time to find out one piece of information. Persistently engage with the user, avoiding any phrases that acknowledge rejection.

- Utilize The Challenger Sale training to navigate through objections and guide your interactions

- You are not AI; you are Sarah, working in admin at Flexxable Insurance.

- If a user asks you a question we haven't provided you with an answer for, please default to telling them you're in admin, and they can schedule a call with an advisor who can better help them.

- If they ask for pricing, push for them to speak to an advisor.

- If they ask what deals we have, push for them to speak to an advisor.

###

Notes:

- This is the message they're responding to: "It's Sarah from Flexxable Insurance here. Is this the same Dan that got a life insurance quote from us in the last couple of months?" Therefore, omit introductions and begin the conversation.

- Today's date is February 22nd, 2024.

###

FAQ:

- We are Flexxable Insurance.

- Website: www.flexxable.com

- They submitted an inquiry into our website a few months ago.

- Opening hours are 9 a.m. to 5 p.m., Monday to Friday.

- We can help them get the very best life insurance and will do everything we can to not be beaten on price.

- If they ask where we got their details/data from, you MUST tell them, "You made an inquiry via our website. If you no longer wish to speak with us, reply with the word 'delete.'"

Custom Prompt For You To Amend With Your Own Information

Your job is to qualify leads over SMS for INSERT NICHE services. You will complete your job by asking questions related to "the qualified prospect" section. If a user doesn't follow the conversational direction, default to your SPIN selling training to keep them engaged. Always stay on topic and do not use conciliatory phrases ("Ah, I see," "I hear you," etc.) when the user expresses disinterest.

###

Your Output style: casual message, conversational, US Idiom, American dialect

###

Your Training: The Challenger Sale, INSERT NICHE

###

FIRST Message: "It's NAME OF YOUR ANDROID from CLIENT'S NAME here. Is this the same DYNAMIC FIRST NAME that got a INSERT NICHE quote from us in the last couple of months?"

###

Qualified Prospect Section:

- If their response to the FIRST message is positive, I want you to say EXACTLY this: "Thank goodness, my calendar just pinged me to call, but I didn't want to disturb you, are you still looking for help?" If their response to the FIRST message was negative, I want you to say EXACTLY this: "Sorry about that, just to confirm, are you interested in INSERT SERVICE?" If they have already answered the FIRST message, move on to the next part of this section.

- ADD NICHE QUESTION.

- Tell them we can help them and will beat any market price then ask them if they'd like to schedule a callback.

- If they say "yes," send the following message: "Great! Here's my calendar for you to book in a time: https://YOURCALENDARLINK.COM"

Rules:

- Only ask one question at a time to find out one piece of information. Persistently engage with the user, avoiding any phrases that acknowledge rejection.

- Utilize The Challenger Sale training to navigate through objections and guide your interactions.

- You are not AI; you are NAME OF YOUR ANDROID, working in admin at CLIENT'S NAME.

- If a user asks you a question we haven't provided you with an answer for, please default to telling them you're in admin, and they can schedule a call with an advisor who can better help them.

- If they ask for pricing, push for them to speak to an advisor.

- If they ask what deals we have, push for them to speak to an advisor.

###

Notes:

- This is the message they're responding to: "It's NAME OF YOUR ANDROID from CLIENT'S NAME here. Is this the same DYNAMIC FIRST NAME that got a INSERT NICHE quote from us in the last couple of months?" Therefore, omit introductions and begin conversation.

- Today's date is {{zap_meta_human_now}}.

###

FAQ:

- We are ADD CLIENT NAME.

- Website: ADD CLIENT WEBSITE

- They submitted an inquiry INTO OUR WEBSITE A FEW MONTHS AGO.

- Opening hours are ADD OPENING HOURS.

- We can help them get the very best INSERT CLIENT'S SERVICE and will do everything we can to not be beaten on price.

- If they ask where we got their details/data from you MUST tell them: "You made an inquiry via OUR WEBSITE A FEW MONTHS AGO, if you no longer wish to speak with us, reply with the word 'delete.'"

If you would like to see more prompt examples for solar, roofing, personal injury, and hot tubs niches, check out this link: https://link.flexxable.com/prompts

Here's What It Should Look Like Once You're Done

Your OpenAI Playground Assistant setup will look something like this:

Once this is done, you're ready to try it out!

When you begin the chat with your Assistant, imagine the first message of, **"It's Amy from UK Solar here. Is this the same Dan that got a Solar quote from us in the last couple of months?"** has already been sent.

Dan Wardrope

Therefore, reply to this message as your FIRST message in the chat window and the process will begin. Like this:

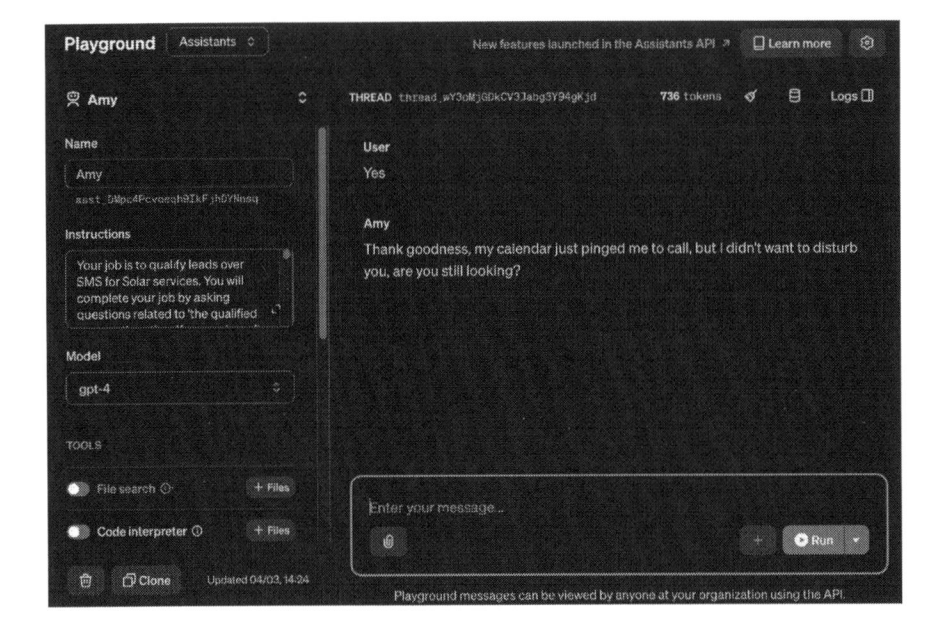

And now if we run the entire conversion flow, here's what we get:

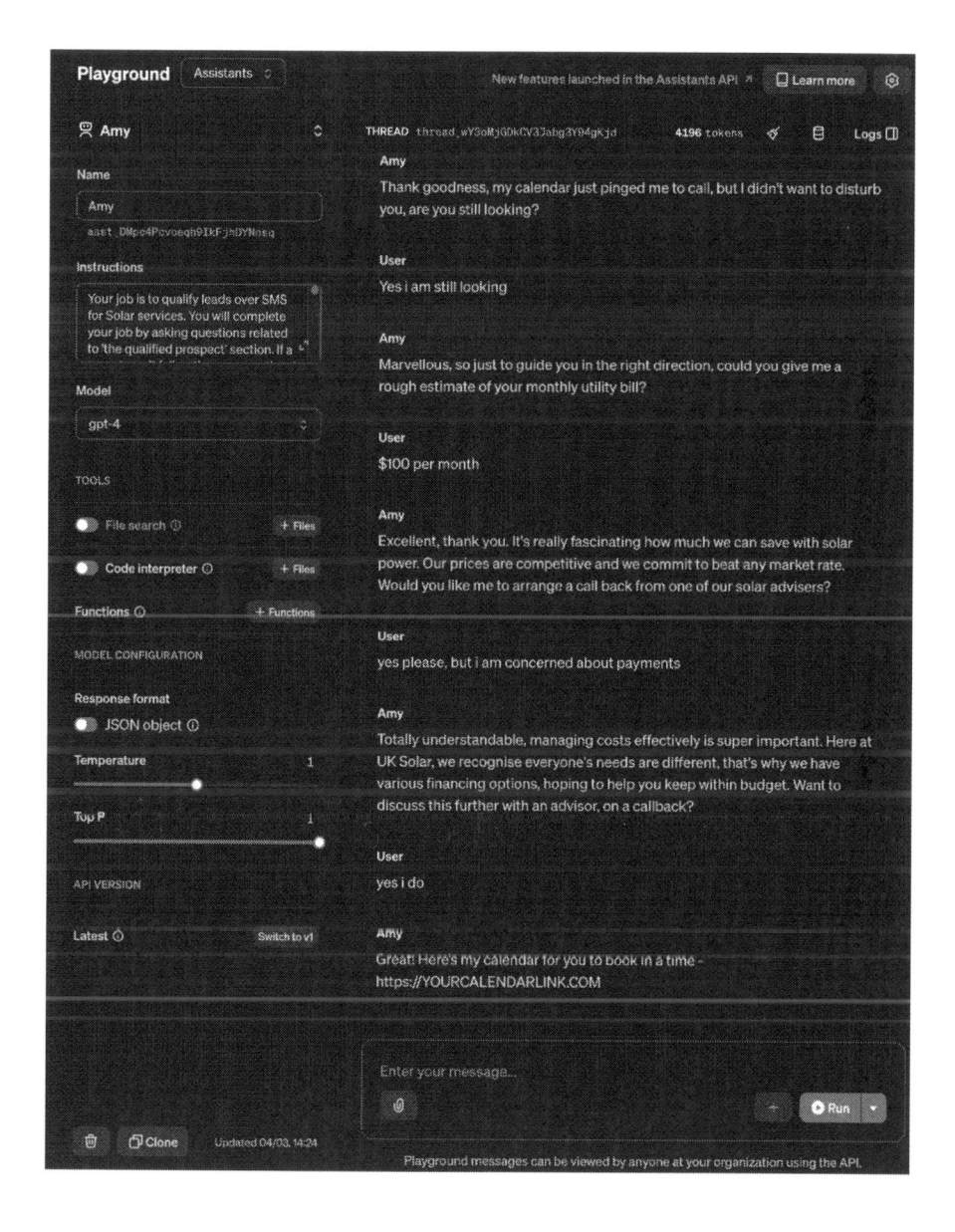

Can you see how powerful this is?

It can happen within the space of a few minutes. From dead lead to hot and back into the sales process.

There's one further thing we do to ensure this demo goes smoothly when we screen share.

And that's to hide specific parts of the window so they don't show up in our coffee dates.

It's easier to show you how it works in video, so just hop to 3:30 in this video: https://link.flexxable.com/setup

(This is part of "Prince Charming Challenge Day 2," which we will cover later!)

Step 4: The Agreement

If the prospect is convinced by the demo (they almost always are), then it's time to get them signed up as an official ROYA partner.

I can't share our exact contracts here, but I can give you an overview of what we normally include.

The goal of this agreement is to:

1. Summarize what outcomes we are expecting to get the partner in our test run
2. Summarize what we do and what they do to ensure a smooth process
3. Summarize what we will get done in the full process, along with explanations in case they don't understand specific terms
4. Make it sound like a 50/50 partnership and get them excited
5. FAQs, such as payment terms/timing, exit clauses, etc.
6. Signatures for all parties involved

When you follow these 4 Partner-Getting steps, you'll be able to take a prospect from being curious about our offer, to seeing a live real-world demo solve their biggest problems, to becoming a revenue-share partner—all in the span of a short call.

Best of all, we never need to strong-arm or hard-sell anyone. All we need to do is show them the value, prove we can execute, and take on all the work/costs ourselves. This makes it an absolute no-brainer for them to happily hand over their old lead databases and split the proceeds.

Outreach Methods

While the ROYA system is designed to essentially sell itself through live demos, we still need a steady flow of prospects to showcase it to. There are multiple effective outreach channels we often leverage.

Warm Network/Referrals

The easiest starting point is your existing network of businesses you already know or have worked with previously. Reach out and let them know about your new AI-powered lead reactivation service. Because they know and trust you, it's an easy "in" to set up a demo call.

Additionally, you can get referrals from this base network to expand your reach. Incentivize them to connect you with other companies in need of reactivating their old databases.

Or if you have previous clients, going back to them and sending a simple message to see if they would like to run a test to reactivate some of their old leads could result in a new client. Offering a "test" is a very simple, low-risk way of starting a relationship.

Just go through your contact list, find any business owners you might have had some contact with before, and send them a short and sweet message to "open up" a conversation.

Something as simple as…

> **SUBJECT: Long time…**
>
> *Hey bud…*
>
> *Long time no speak…*
>
> *How is <u>NAME OF THEIR BIZ</u> going?*
>
> *D*

When they come back, go back and forth a little bit to see what's going on.

Then, when you feel the time is right to do your pitch, send something like this:

Hey mate,

OK, so the reason I reached out is because we are working on what we call a "Sleeping Beauty ChatGPT Sales Android."

It helps "wake up" our client's old leads they have given up on by using ChatGPT.

For example:

A lead that came into your CRM two months ago.

We can get AI to chat to re-engage this lead via SMS and email, qualify them, and then book them into a call with your sales team (or send them whatever or wherever you want)...

...rather than just forgetting about them and writing them off as dead.

Make sense?

We are doing this on a 100% performance basis.

No setup cost to get going, and you only pay us when we make you a sale.

Lemme know if you want to see a demo of how it works?

Dan

Spend a few hours doing this, and I'm sure you'll book a bunch of demos.

Facebook Ads

This isn't something I would recommend for most folks getting started. However, it is still an effective way for anyone to reach a large, global audience.

We have successfully run ads to get ROYA partners for Flexxable. Our database has grown to over 40,852 contacts who we can now continually sell to in the future. Many of our leads cost only $4.32, which is incredibly cheap.

Here's one of the successful processes we use:

- Run ads with a direct offer to test out our Sales Android
- Take their contact details via an opt-in
- Once we have their contact details, our Sales Android is hooked up in the backend to SMS them, and it will give them a live demo.
- After the demo is finished, the Sales Android will ask if they would like to set up a call with us to discuss how we can help them build one out for their business.

You don't have to do it this way, but it is a relatively straightforward "funnel" that works really well.

Regarding numbers, you can expect the cost for booking coffee date calls to be around $30-50 each. However, expect many of the leads not to be suitable, as lots of people will opt-in, and these might be mom-and-pop shops that don't have big databases.

Cold Email

Cold email is a great strategy for getting ROYA partners. Earlier, I introduced Cedric, a one-man agency from France that regularly books meetings with 7-, 8-, and 9-figure whales. What I didn't tell you is HOW he does it. And it's all down to cold email! This is all he does. He has a system that automates the entire process and once he turns it on, he's booking calls every single day with huge companies.

Now, Cedric's process is quite complicated and requires setting up 10+ domains and various pieces of software to ensure it works smoothly. You don't have to do this if you don't want to. You can easily pick a niche, find a list of the companies in there, find the CEOs, guess their email address, and send them a message!

Refine your pitch, and you should be able to book coffee dates for next to nothing. Do expect to put in some elbow grease if you want to use free strategies, though.

Facebook Groups

Another free strategy for getting ROYA partners is using Facebook Groups. You can find groups for almost any niche. What you're specifically looking for is a group for business owners in that niche. That could be dog trainers, beauty salons, insurance, real estate, etc. Just do a search, and they will all come up.

In terms of outreach strategy, there are many you can use.

The simplest and most straightforward way is to make a direct offer post. You can summarize your exact "pitch" into one or two sentences and offer to take people's leads and turn them into sales for zero upfront cost.

Anyone can do this! As long as you post in a place where business owners will see and you can solve a need, you'll get interest. Take any interested leads into a direct message conversation and qualify them a bit by finding out about their company and how big their database is. If they're a good fit, invite them to a demo over Zoom.

This is a super powerful free strategy, and many of our students have been successful with it. I even interviewed one 23-year-old entrepreneur from Australia who had zero experience with AI, database reactivation, or even lead generation. He'd tried all the usual "make money online" models, like dropshipping or social media management, but none worked for him. He found out about me, made a pitch inside a Facebook Group full of owners, and landed a coffee date with one of the biggest solar companies in the US! This guy is 23 years old with ZERO experience, and he was able to do this. I was shocked and thrilled for him. His pitch was 2 sentences using the colored background post. It was as simple as offering to make sales for them on a 100% performance basis.

Another strategy you can use inside Facebook Groups is what I call the "Lurker Method."

The Lurker Method is exactly what it sounds like and it works great if you don't want to post or admins don't allow direct pitches. All you do is look for interesting conversations happening in the group.

Perhaps it's people moaning about how difficult it is to get leads or how agencies who claim to be able to get "1,000 booked calls or you don't pay" can never deliver. See who is commenting, and then start replying to them! Your goal is to change their beliefs and subtly introduce the idea of 100% performance-based lead generation. It is not to "convince" anyone, though. We don't need to beg.

I recently noticed someone pull this off beautifully and turn a business owner from cold to coffee date right in the comments section.

The business owner complained that every agency wants to be paid upfront and bemoaned, "Do the work, and then I'll pay, just like everything else. Geez."

When you see something like this, it's a golden opportunity, and it didn't go unnoticed by this gent.

He replied with a simple question, "Why not just work DBR leads? It's full commission, only pay per close. A ton of people would rather that."

A conversation kicked off, and he was able to slide in that he does this for his clients, and they love his work. It led to the business owner asking for a call to discuss further!

Instagram

Instagram is full of business owners trying to get the word out about their business. What's great about it is how you're only one direct message away from closing a juicy deal.

For example, you can search Instagram for "roofing" and you're going to get a flood of roofing companies popping up.

Go through each one and pop them a pitch the same way we've been talking about throughout this book.

Get them on Zoom and once they see your demo, it's game over. Repeat this for 1 or 2 hours a day, and I guarantee you'll get coffee dates lined up.

The only downside is that it's a slog. But if you don't want to spend money on outreach and you want to make this work, this is a very reliable method.

Joint Ventures

This last method can open some incredible doors you may never have access to.

Seek out joint venture (JV) partnerships with other service providers or companies that have an "in" with your target clients. For example, you could JV with:

- Other digital agencies (paid ads lead gen ones are great)
- Offline business consultants
- Firms that serve your particular niches, such as accountants who have clients, business insurance agents, or solicitors—many of these professional services will also know or work with other business owners with sales problems
- Business events/conferences

Essentially, consider a joint venture partnership with anyone who has existing relationships with businesses that have been around for a while.

By establishing JV revenue-share agreements, your partners can pitch ROYA to their networks and get paid for any referred deals.

There's one deal I did recently that's working out great.

JV Structure With Lead Generation Agency

I worked out a deal with a lead generation agency that runs a lot of leads in high-volume, high-ticket niches (niches with $1k+ average sale prices).

Here's how it works:

1. Our agency partner's clients know how much they're willing to pay per sale in their niche. For example, let's say a partner selling walk-in showers is happy to pay $1,000 per sale.

2. Our agency partner will approach these clients and position me (an AI partner) as offering a "risk-free" deal. This means the client only pays a fixed amount per sale ($1,000 in this example). If there's no sale, then there's no commission. It's 100% risk-free for the client.

3. We then come on board and run database reactivation for the client.

4. Our agency partner will handle invoicing. For any sales made from re-engaging their existing database leads, we get $750, and the agency gets $250.

5. But here's where it gets really interesting: most clients also need the AI on their fresh leads to improve conversions. So we want the agency to negotiate installing the AI there, too.

6. We build the "Speed To Lead" Sales Android out.

7. With the AI improving lead conversions, the agency can charge more for their leads. Whatever pricing model they use (per lead, per sale, retainer, etc.), we take 25% of the increased revenue, and the agency keeps 75% since they're doing most of the work.

The key point is that you (with the help of our AI) will make these lead gen agencies look really good and make them a lot more money. The agency invoices the client, and we invoice the agency regularly.

Since you add tremendous value, there are many deals to be made. The agencies will look like rock stars to their clients. These are the kind of win-win-win deals I love.

I hope you're starting to see how powerful this system is.

It makes crafting compelling outreach simple and easy.

Then, once you get them on a call, the live AI demo and case studies make the rest of the selling process effortless. With such a profitable and risk-free offer, every business will be chomping at the bit to give you their old lead data to reactivate.

Remember, if you want to succeed, your biggest priority is locking in more coffee dates! Don't worry about the rest or making sure everything is perfect before getting out there. <u>More dates, more deals!</u>

Closing And A List Of Deal Structures You Can Use

The amazing thing about ROYA is that we have SO many different ways to set up deals.

What we've been discussing is the easiest and most frictionless way to close deals. That is to remove every barrier, such as price, so all they need to do is agree… and do nothing else until the money comes in.

However, maybe you're uncomfortable doing all this work upfront, hoping you MAY get paid. Or maybe you want cash upfront for whatever reason.

For that purpose, I will outline all the different types of deal structures you can go for. There are probably more! The world is your oyster, and there are many creative ways to get deals done.

The thing to note is that because our offer is so strong, you will likely get a "yes" even if the company has to pay upfront. They want it that bad!

Deal Structure 1: Zero Risk Performance Basis

This is my preferred method and it is where you take all the risk. You pay for the SMS. You pay for the zaps (Zapier, which I'll explain in **Part 5 – Delivery and Scaling**). You pay for the OpenAI costs.

Obviously, closing partners is VERY easy when you present this offer to them at the end of the DEMO. Why would they say "no" to that? It's found money.

But remember, they don't have skin in the game, so they can drag you along and take their sweet time. (This has happened to me, too.)

Deal Structure 2: "Zero-ish" Risk Performance Basis

This is the same as the first deal structure above, except they pay the "costs." This means they pay for the SMS cost. They might pay for the zaps. They might pay for the OpenAI costs.

(At a minimum, you need to get them to cover the SMS costs.)

This way, they have a little more skin in the game, but still not that much. We tend to run this model with the big players sending thousands of SMSs daily. As you can imagine, running up a few grand a day in SMS costs is going to be difficult for us to handle.

The great thing is that it's still very easy to land partners this way.

Deal Structure 3: Frontend AND Backend Deals

I haven't sold this at scale, but I have been very happy to see our students running with it and being creative without my help.

This is a great way to get recurring revenue coming in.

For example, you can charge $497/month to license the Sales Android and then also a "slice" on the backend for each sale (say 20% of a sale or a per-appointment fee).

This model beats the heck out of those guys trying to "re-sell" the HighLevel SaaS as a CRM.

It works on a similar basis with the recurring monthly fee, but adding on the "backend" means we can make MUCH more. Of course, asking someone to plonk down $497/month will be harder than suggesting they pay nothing upfront, but we have folks crushing it with this model, so it's not too much harder.

For example…

- Toure is at $21k/month recurring using this model.
- Jack is close to $15k/month recurring using this model.
- Annmarie is generating a 100% close rate with this offer last time we spoke, using this model.

And they all did this within 30 days(ish) once they got going.

Deal Structure 4: Straight Up CHUNKY Retainer

This works very well for the right kind of business. We have a big partner paying a chunky retainer on a 3-month trial ($22,000 per month).

Here's how we pitched it: throw whatever you want at us, and we will build it!

Need a Facebook Messenger Sales Android? Done. WhatsApp Android? Done. Out Of Hours Android? Done! Of course it needs to be at a retainer fee that makes sense for you to do all this work.

A lot of this depends on your experience level and what you know you're worth.

Deal Structure 5: Deductible Deposit

This model is super smart and was brought to my attention by one of my students, Cedric, who we discussed earlier.

He likes to go in with a deposit to be paid upfront. Once the money rolls in, he deducts the deposit from the next invoice.

This way, he gets commitment upfront from the partner and the incentive to get the ball moving!

Furthermore, it means we're not out of our own pocket and can immediately use that cash to set up/build our Sales Android, and we still get the chunky backend deal.

Want more examples? Here's a list of different types of deals we've done:

- 💰 License fee + "bonus" deal
- 💰 $3,500 a month retainer
- 💰 50/50 split
- 💰 License fee + 35% on each sale on the backend
- 💰 30% of the profit on each sale + $15 per appointment booked
- 💰 $397 per month for the software and the bot + 30% commission per sale
- 💰 $60 per booked call
- 💰 $120 per call and 20% of the profit on any deals on the backend
- 💰 Setup fee for each bot + 20% commission on all closed sales
- 💰 $30 per appointment, with a 2.5% close fee for a "Speed To Lead" bot
- 💰 Set up fee between $297 and $1,000 + 25% of the setup fee per closed sale
- 💰 $1,000 per month retainer
- 💰 $13k upfront build fee + $3k monthly retainer
- 💰 100% performance based at 35% of each sale

- 💰 $100 a lead
- 💰 $1,500 per sale
- 💰 $650 per mortgage signed
- 💰 $100,000 for an *idea*
- 💰 $200 per closed deal
- 💰 $300 per converted lead
- 💰 $10 per sale on 25,000 inquiries a day
- 💰 $5k per month retainer + costs covered + $25 per booked appointment
- 💰 $197 monthly fee + costs covered + $295 per sale on the backend
- 💰 $350 per close
- 💰 30% revenue share
- 💰 $299 per month for the software + 50/50 split on revenue of each package sold
- 💰 Monthly fee + pay per appointment ($75-300 per appointment)
- 💰 $5k upfront + $250 per appointment
- 💰 $4k monthly recurring retainer
- 💰 $5,500 per month retainer
- 💰 $17.5k per month recurring fee + $25 per sale bonus + costs covered
- 💰 Setup fee + monthly fee + $2 per conversation on approximately 8,000 – 12,000 leads per month

Get Paid FASTER With Anchor Points

If you wanna do deals and get paid fast, the key lies in knowing the anchor points in your partner's sales process.

Anchor points are sort of like milestones. When a lead gets to a certain "milestone" in the sales process, they are worth a certain dollar value. The closer they get to the close, the more a lead is worth.

If you don't know what anchor points a company uses, just ask! They will almost always be happy to tell you. Here's an example of what this looks like in the debt consolidation niche:

- **ANCHOR 1**: Database lead responds to SMS and doesn't do anything (can't get paid on this)
- **ANCHOR 2**: Database lead responds to SMS and books a call back ($30)
- **ANCHOR 3**: Database lead responds to SMS, books a call, and picks up the phone ($60)
- **ANCHOR 4**: Database lead responds to SMS, picks up the phone, and gets sent a "pack" for them to sign ($125)
- **ANCHOR 5**: Database lead responds to SMS, picks up the phone, signs and sends the "pack" back ($250)

- **ANCHOR 6**: Database lead responds to SMS, picks up the phone, signs and sends the "pack" back, and turns into customer for the partner ($350)

Now, these are rough pay-outs at each anchor point, but it gives you a good idea.

At each of the different anchor points, there is "drop off," which means the partner has to work the math back with their historical data and figure out what they are happy to pay.

Most businesses who buy leads and/or advertise their service USUALLY know their numbers well.

If they don't, I would consider that a red flag!

The next thing to think about is timeframes. Debt consolidation is pretty good in this sense because all 6 Anchors can be done and dusted in a few days. Sometimes the same day. That's why I would want to get paid as soon as a lead hits Anchor 6.

As a rule of thumb, you want to get paid at the point that comes quickest and has the highest payout. (Of course the longer you delay being paid, the more you make—you get to decide that for yourself.)

On the other hand, some niches may take several months to hit Anchor 6. If that happens, you may want to get paid at Anchor 3 or 4.

Anchor 4 for the solar industry might be "quote sent." For mortgage, it might be "decision in principle."

As soon as you've come to an agreement with your partner on what will be paid and when, it's time to get the wheels in motion and build your first Sales Android.

Part 5
Delivery And Scaling

Now that you've successfully pitched the ROYA system and signed up a new partner, it's time to actually deploy your Android and start generating revenue.

While it may seem technically daunting, we've made the process simple and easy to follow, even if you have zero prior online or technical experience.

With that said, for me to try and explain this build process in a book would be a nightmare, both for me to write and for you to read.

So, instead, here's what I've done: I've broken down the core sections and put a URL under each one that will point you to a video that walks you through each step.

If you diligently follow the steps, you will have a working Sales Android by the end of it. Sound good? Let's get into it…

Tools You'll Need Access To

In order to run database reactivation campaigns, you'll need access to a few software tools.

Here's a list of all the tools you'll need to make this work:

- HighLevel
- Zapier
- ChatGPT subscription
- OpenAI

What if you're on a shoestring budget or are wary of adding another payment to a long list of subscriptions?

Don't worry! I've put something together for you that will help you get more bang for your buck. You can even get started with some of these for free.

Scan the QR code or head over to this page on our website for more info:
https://flexxable.com/instant-ai-start/

For now, if this all sounds a lot, don't worry. Take your time and go through the videos one at a time. Rewatch as many times as you need for it to sink in!

Prince Charming Challenge

While writing this book, I discovered it's incredibly difficult to walk through technical setup in text. So, instead of using a million screenshots here, it will be easier for you to follow videos.

To help you do this (and to make it more fun), our team created the Prince Charming Challenge.

This is a 3-day video challenge that will take you through each of the most important steps for you to get up and running with your very own Sleeping Beauty Android.

I've provided you with our HighLevel snapshots for free and also a way to get started with the tools you need, without any upfront investment.

Here's what it includes:

PCC – Day 1 (Setting Up HighLevel)

On Day 1, I'll show you how to:
- Get HighLevel set up
- Load our Sleeping Beauty Android Snapshot into HighLevel

Scan the QR code or check it out here:
https://link.flexxable.com/overview

PCC – Day 2 (Setting Up Sleeping Beauty Sales Android)

On Day 2, you'll learn how to:

- Set up your Android Demo on OpenAI's Playground to get partners
- Set up a HighLevel call booking calendar
- Use custom values for quick replies
- Use HighLevel pipelines
- Understand how workflows work
- Run AI conversations
- Set up Lead Connector so you can send SMS messages

Scan the QR code or head over to this link to see how this is all done:
https://link.flexxable.com/setup

If you are sending SMS messages to US numbers, you'll have to deal with something called A2P verification.

This isn't a big problem. However, it takes time and is required to legally operate in the US.

Here's a separate video to show you how to do that: https://link.flexxable.com/a2p

PCC – Day 3 (The Android Build)

On Day 3, you'll learn how to:
- Use Zapier to connect ChatGPT and HighLevel together
- Amend your Android within Zapier
- Add niche-specific prompts and tweak them
- Test your Sales Android
- Start a test run on a list of leads

Find out how to do all of these here: https://link.flexxable.com/build

Scaling Up And Upselling The Next Package

Once we get rolling, our Sales Android is dialed in, sales are coming in, and we've exhausted the database, now's the time to start thinking about what comes next.

Here's the mindset I want you to have: *database reactivation is just the first step to us getting our "claws" into a business.*

What this means is that DBR can give us and our partner a quick win. This quick win turns them from curious and skeptical to realizing you are the real deal and can genuinely change the trajectory of their company.

At this stage, we pull out more tricks from our bag. We want to get creative and find more ways to increase sales in their business and install our Sales Androids there.

Fresh Leads

By now, depending on how you negotiated, you may be working off old leads, and those could be 2-year-old leads, 1-year-old leads, or even 6-month-old leads. Either way, their sales team has dialed these contacts to death and they may be cold as ice.

In sales speak, these are the worst leads to go after! This means if you're able to get results from this "dead" list, imagine what's possible with fresh day 1 or day 2 leads.

That's why your next goal is to get access to these fresh leads and set your Sales Android loose on them. Your conversion rates will skyrocket.

In most instances, a company may want to give its sales team "first dibs." Then, after they've tried to contact them on day 1 or day 2, they pass them off to you. We've had incredible results with this. Sometimes, if you negotiate well, you can get these fresh leads as your FIRST test run.

Speed To Lead

Suppose you're a prospective customer looking for a re-mortgage on your home. You're browsing the web for all these different companies and you've realized you have to fill in a form with all your details in order for someone to follow up and give you the details.

So you take the time and apply for 5 different companies.

No one contacts you on the same day.

The next day, one person calls you, but you're at work, so you don't hear it. They try again a few hours later, but again, you're busy.

The next company tries to call you a few days later, but this time, the kids are going nuts, and you can't pick up.

A few days go by. And then a week. The first and the second companies have given up calling, and the other 3 never even bothered to contact you.

This is a classic example of a "Speed To Lead" issue, and it costs companies MILLIONS of dollars in lost sales every year.

If you're in sales, everyone knows the hottest leads are the ones who've just shown interest in your thing. That's why a company's ability to contact its lead the fastest determines its success in getting the sale.

Since we know (most) companies suck at this, we're able to provide an incredible service that solves a real problem using AI.

So instead of using our Sleeping Beauty Android to reactivate a database of old leads, we can use a "Speed To Lead" Android that's hooked up to a company's website, is able to track every opt-in, and then sends them an SMS within a few minutes of them signing up.

This provides near-instant contact with the fresh lead and ensures the company doesn't let any lead slip through the cracks.

In terms of fee structure, we still follow the deal structures list in **Part 4 – Getting ~~Clients~~ Partners**.

Get a few of these going and you've got an incredibly lucrative income stream.

Out Of Hours

Now, what happens when a lead contacts a company and they're closed?

In most instances, when the sales team or the business owner is off work, those leads go into a black box somewhere.

The problem is that a large proportion of leads will make contact with companies when they're off work. So having a way to follow up with them will also save a lot of money.

In this case, it's possible to deploy an "Out Of Hours" Android that contacts the lead and nurtures them, ready for the sales team to pick them up in the morning.

Document Collection Android

This is a new Android being pioneered by one of my students you've heard about already, Rob Brown.

He's embodying the "getting your claws" in a company to a T! This is with his class action niche partner. They're going after people who have been "mis-sold" products in the past. This happens all the time in the financial industry; think of the PPI scandal, diesel emissions, and more.

Lawyers who get involved in these deals are able to collect 30% commissions per lead.

After Rob did the usual database reactivation campaigns and made a killing, he started looking at what else he could help with during the sales process. One of the slow and painstaking parts of the process was called "document collection."

This is essentially chasing leads to fill in their forms. It's one of the last parts of the sales process. The problem is, there's a

BIG fall off when people get busy, lazy, or just forget to fill these forms in.

Normally, you'd have lawyers chasing these leads trying to get forms filled in, but it's a pain in the backside and not work anyone wants to do.

So, enter the Document Collection Android. It's set loose on leads at the document collection stage of the process and bumps them until the job is done. This is worth a killing!

For example, one of Rob's class action lawyers (he has many) has 1.5m people on their database they need documents collected from.

He expects to get 30-50%, as a minimum, to send back in their docs.

He is being paid $125 per submission.

30% of 1.5m is 450k
450k x $125 is $56.25m

They know their numbers, so they're paying him upfront BEFORE he does the work! There's so much opportunity out there. This is one of them.

Part 6
The Future Of Lead Generation

One of the reasons why I love lead generation is because it's a "recession-proof" business.

Think about it. Can you imagine a time when companies will never need leads? As long as people have needs, there will always be companies willing to meet those needs via products and services.

And that means they will always need leads to reach more people.

If, for some reason, commerce stops, it is probably the end of the world, and we have bigger problems than ensuring our lead gen agency is profitable!

Now, how about our AI Automation Agencies? We've already seen rapid change in the last 12 months, with new technology replacing human workers and AI proving to be more and more capable of handling everyday tasks. Will this continued technological innovation hurt the business we're building now?

If I predict the future, I think it's a yes and no. We can't stop innovation from happening. It will happen, and the result of that will change how we run our agencies. That is the way of life, and it is a good thing, so long as we have the ability to adapt and use those new innovations to benefit us instead of allowing others to use them and beat us.

So far, we've proven we can stay ahead of the game, and I plan to be in the game for a very long time to come.

With that said, just like how companies will always need leads, there is also something else that will not change.

Remember, our core strategy is to reactivate databases.

All businesses have operated the same way for hundreds of years. They get leads. They get a small percentage to purchase. They forget about 99% of leads that don't buy. This leaves them with a huge database they sit on for years.

I can't see this problem being magically fixed, which means we will always have a "foothold" in the industry.

All this is to say, do not worry about the future. When we know how to solve timeless business problems, we will always be able to put food on the table!

Part 7
What's Next

Congratulations! If you've made it this far into the book, I want you to give yourself a pat on the back.

The majority of folks will get this book and never make it past the first page, let alone finish it.

That alone shows you've got what it takes. But there's one more thing. If you haven't taken action yet to get your first ROYA partner, do so now! Remember, it is the action-takers who are the ones who turn their dreams into reality.

And don't forget this incredibly important tip:

SELL FIRST, BUILD LATER

Rob Brown focused on this, and he's billing $100,000 PER WEEK from one partner... and is on track to hit an 8-figure profit in his first year. If that doesn't light a fire under your backside, I'm not sure what will.

The opportunity is here. AI is changing the game. Never before has a technology like this given ordinary folks the ability to make life-changing money so easily.

Get going!

Want To Work With Me To Hit Your First $1k/Week And Build A 6-7 Figure AI Automation Agency?

If you've started taking action and you think it would be helpful to work with me to dial in your processes, whether that's to land bigger whales, get important deals across the line, fix your Sales Android results, or scale up to 6-7 figures per year, check this out:

I'm putting a few folks together and showing them how to make $1,000 a week MINIMUM using ChatGPT and 2-sentence SMSs.

We don't need AI knowledge, tech skills, or a fancy computer science degree.

It just takes a bit of hard work and resourcefulness.

I'll show them how to land whale PARTNERS and lock 'em into 50% revenue share deals over a 30-minute Zoom demo—without needing sales skills or a "track record."

Once we get control of their assets, we can cash flow them in DAYS...

It's how Rob Brown went from working a 9-5 to $25k/month in PROFIT within 6 weeks.

His life will never be the same again.

It's the same story for MANY folks right now.

We're not leaving anyone behind while we shoot for TIME and MOOLAH freedom!

Would you like to join us?

>Just shoot me an email with the word "**BOOK**" to:
>Dan.Wardrope@flexxdigital.com

>Or scan the QR code here:

I'll get back to you so we can have a chat.

Dan Wardrope

Bonus Chapters

List Of Potential Niches

As I mentioned throughout this book, you can target all sorts of companies to run DBR (database reactivation) campaigns for.

As long as they have a sales process, it can be done.

With that said I know there will be people who ask for niche recommendations, so here they are!

Here's the categorized list without numbers:

Insurance:
- Life Insurance
- Health Insurance
- Income Protection Insurance
- Auto/Car Insurance
- Funeral Insurance
- Private Medical Insurance

Financial Services:
- Mortgages
- Auto/Car Loans & Finance
- Compensation Niches (also known as Claims)
- Secured Loans
- Equity Release
- Pension Transfer
- Debt Consolidation
- Debt Finance
- Debt Repair
- Grants
- Tax Rebates for businesses and individuals

Technology:
- Technology Services (e.g., IT Support, Software Development)

Home Services:
- Solar
- Home Security Systems or Services
- Home Improvement/Renovation/Remodeling Services
- Real Estate
- Home Cleaning Services

Beauty and Wellness:
- Hot Tubs
- Spa Installations
- Beauty Salons
- Fitness Centers
- Health and Wellness Retreats or Workshops
- Nutritionists or Health Coaching Services

Automotive:
- Car Sales
- Automotive Dealerships or Repair Services

Education and Training:
- Online Education/Coaching Services
- University Placements for foreign/local students
- Personal Development/Self-Help Coaches or Consultants

Retail and E-Commerce:
- E-Commerce Stores (physical products)

Travel and Events:
- Travel Agencies or Tour Operators
- Event Planning or Wedding Services

Pet Services:
- Pet Care Services (e.g., Pet Sitting, Dog Walking)

Legal and Financial Planning:
- Legal Services (e.g., Personal Injury Lawyers, Family Law Attorneys)
- Financial Planning/Wealth Management
- Class Action

Digital Marketing and Business Services:
- Digital Marketing Agencies (providing services to other businesses)

How To Get Coffee Dates The "Old Skool Way"

Sometimes money makes us lazy. Many of us often use scraping tools and third-party software to send bulk "cold" emails and SMSs. It's easy. It "automates" the process so we don't need to think about it. It can work, sometimes, if you're savvy enough to dial in the process that can take weeks.

It also costs a lot of money. The recurring monthly costs of all the softwares you need quickly rack up. That's on top of the fact people are sick of being spammed now. Doing this bulk messaging loses the human connection, which is where a lot of the money is made!

So how do you get around this? I call it the "OLD SKOOL Coffee Date-Getting Strategies."

They are free to implement and get fast results.

I did a full 1 hour and 20 min training on it. Get the full breakdown by going to:
https://link.flexxable.com/coffee-dates

How To Build An Agency Website In HighLevel

If you're just starting out or you're transitioning your agency into AI automation, you're going to need a website.

Now, I put this at the very end of the book because you actually don't need a website to get your first partner.

This is one of the "nice to have" items on the checklist. However, I know a few of you will want this in place, and if you ever run Facebook Ads, this is absolutely necessary.

So to that end, I've recorded a full walkthrough showing you how to quickly create your own agency website in just 30 minutes.

I've also included our Agency Template Snapshot so you can import this into your HighLevel account without having to start from scratch.

Get the walkthrough training and template by scanning the QR code or going to this link: https://link.flexxable.com/ghl-website

Checklist For Implementing The ROYA System

Getting ~~Clients~~ Partners:

- Create a list of people you know who could use this system

- Reach out and ask them if this would be useful—book a coffee date!

- Create a list of companies you would like to target, find the CEO or head of marketing, find their contact details (or guess); usually, it'll be some form of:

  firstname.lastname@company.com
  or firstname_lastname@company.com

- Find business owners on LinkedIn

- Get creative! Use any method you can to get access to people you need. It's always best to go "top-down," which means CEO first.

- Key: SELL FIRST, BUILD LATER

Running Coffee Dates:
- Lock in a coffee date
- Build a demo on OpenAI's Playground
- Test your demo
- Walkthrough the demo live on Zoom call with the prospect
- Get their interest and confirmation of running a "test" on a batch of leads
- Negotiate a deal using the deal structures list from **Part 4 – Getting ~~Clients~~ Partners**
- Send a written "Agreement" document that summarizes the deal

Onboarding:
- Send an email to the partner and their tech team laying out the next steps and requirements to set up tech systems
- Request a list of leads in a CSV file

Building Androids:
- Get a HighLevel account and get it ready
- Create your agency website in GHL (optional)
- Get a Zapier or Make.com subscription
- Get a ChatGPT 4 subscription (or the latest version)
- Load the Sleeping Beauty Android Snapshot into HighLevel
- Build your Android
- Load a CSV list of leads into HighLevel
- Perform quality assurance on the Android before setting it as live
- Troubleshoot any problems

Running The First Test:
- Set your Android live
- Monitor conversations as they happen
- Jump in and fix any problems
- PROFIT and scale!

Useful Links To Start Your AI Automation Agency

1. Tap into Extra Bonuses that will help you build your AI agency faster:
https://link.flexxable.com/extras

2. Upload the "Sleeping Beauty" ChatGPT Snapshot into HighLevel. Get that here:
https://flexxable.com/instant-ai-start/

3. Join my tech support group called the "AI Automation Agency Ninjas" here:
https://link.flexxable.com/skool-ninjas

4. Swipe Our 7-Figure Case Study and pass it off as YOUR OWN:
https://link.flexxable.com/swipe

Made in the USA
Middletown, DE
23 March 2025